Tricky Punctuation in Cartoons

Lidia Stanton

Illustrated by Sophie Kennedy

Jessica Kingsley Publishers
London and Philadelphia

First published in 2020
by Jessica Kingsley Publishers
73 Collier Street
London N1 9BE, UK

www.jkp.com

Library of Congress Cataloging in Publication Data
A CIP catalog record for this book is available from the Library of Congress

British Library Cataloguing in Publication Data
A CIP catalogue record for this book is available from the British Library

ISBN 978 1 78775 402 7
eISBN 978 1 78775 403 4

Printed and bound in Great Britain

For Lucas,
not because his writing wasn't perfect,
but because it *was*.

Contents

Introduction to Educators and Parents

Correct punctuation:
the difference between
a sentence that's well-written
and a sentence that's, well, written.

Anonymous

Why another reference guide?

This book does not aspire to be another English language reference guide. Its purpose is to make the correct use of punctuation marks achievable for those who rarely use them in places other than the end of a sentence. The book's humour-packed content is designed to be easily processed and hard to put down. References to social media humour make it relevant to young people's everyday experience of electronic literacy.

Most of all, the book's aim is to demystify a belief that punctuation, like spelling and grammar, is difficult to learn if one does not have strong academic skills, is less of a logical thinker, or has a specific learning difficulty, such as dyslexia. Punctuation does make a lot of sense, but that may not be obvious to someone who does not find traditional SPAG (spelling, punctuation and grammar) classroom instruction or reference guides helpful. This book hopes to ignite, or re-ignite, curiosity about punctuation that might have been lost on some academic journeys.

Who is this book for?

The book is for anyone, but should particularly help learners in Key Stage 2 and 3 (aged 9–15) who:

- prefer to learn by seeing and doing, not extensive reading and/or listening
- have tried traditional SPAG strategies but with limited success
- find it difficult to remember and generalise punctuation rules

- have attentional difficulty and/or poor sequential processing skills
- have dyslexia or other specific learning difficulty (SpLD).

I have used the multisensory strategies (building blocks for complex and compound sentences, thumbs for possessive apostrophes, and folded paper for contracting apostrophes) with Year 5 (aged 9–10) and Year 6 (aged 10–11) children, who worked very enthusiastically and were certainly not too young to grasp the complexities of written English language.

If introduced at any point during Key Stage 3, the book can support effective GCSE revision. In the words of the parents of a student I tutored, 'the penny has to drop' before the learner has the confidence to engage with structured SPAG tasks.

How does the book work?

The book assists in development of punctuation skills via enquiry-based learning (also known as problem-based learning), where cartoons are problems to work out in order to understand how punctuation works, and also to make the reader smile. The humorous drawings make the book a visual guide that demands immediate focus and provides humour. Most importantly, the cartoons assist readers in working out punctuation problems themselves before referring to written summaries of rules.

Humour is a kind of play used in the book to challenge the learner's way of thinking about punctuation. Unexpected punch lines suddenly make the dreaded subject funny, thus less daunting. Continuous elements of surprise strengthen the process of self-discovery and consolidate learning when 'Aha!' moments are shared, the way jokes are passed around. The student does not need to read the book 'from cover to cover' but can dip in and out, as they would treat a traditional joke book.

Tricky Punctuation in Cartoons is a visual guide and workbook in one. It encourages a flexible approach to working with punctuation rules, shifting the focus away from deductive to inductive learning. This bottom-up approach enables the learner to move from something specific to more general, to detect patterns from examples and to infer rules. Instead of a rule-driven approach, it is a rule-discovery one. Using problem-based learning, the learner gradually becomes proficient in generalising their new knowledge onto other areas of literacy. Without abandoning elements of deductive teaching altogether, in order to help consolidate newly discovered knowledge, summaries and additional explanations are provided in text boxes.

English and SEN teachers are likely to agree that it is not possible to teach punctuation marks without placing them within the context of grammatical structures. In the second part of the book, alongside implicit humour, concrete props are introduced in the form of building blocks, the student's hands and folded paper. These have positive association with play that effectively bridges the gap between the concrete and more abstract contents. The book replaces the auditory/oral instruction with a visual/practical one, putting the student in control, particularly those with SpLD/dyslexia. The Answer Key at the end of the book is available to download from www.jkp.com/catalogue/book/9781787754027.

The book is not a structured literacy programme. It does not replace any part of current literacy instruction at school. It is intended to complement it to equip the learners with additional ways to remember tricky punctuation rules.

1
Why We Need Punctuation

Are you sitting comfortably? Then I'll... Actually, Zed, my robot assistant, will read you a story.

THANKS FOR HELPING BILLY GET OUT OF THE HOUSE

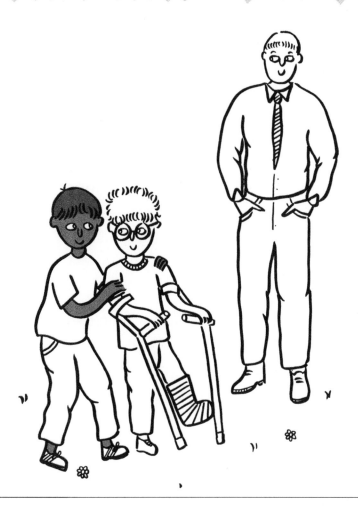

Thanks for helping Billy get out of the house.

Wait! That's a wrong story. Billy is not a boy and he definitely doesn't have a leg in plaster. Billy is a mad dog that always gets into trouble.

Thanks for helping, Billy. Get out of the house!

 STOP AND THINK
How did Zed mix the two stories?

It read the two sentences as one because it didn't see the full stop. It didn't read the comma or exclamation mark, either.

YOU CANT READ PUNCTUATION MARKS

Ah... They are not words, but they tell us a lot about the sentence we are reading. Punctuation might still be a problem for robots but shouldn't be for humans. As soon as children become readers, they know when to change their voice depending on the punctuation mark they see in the sentence.

WHY ROBOTS STRUGGLE TO READ LIKE HUMANS

The human voice can go up and down – we call that **intonation**.

We also use our hands and arms, and move heads during speaking – this is called **gesticulation** (because we use gestures). The challenge is to teach robots to use believable intonation and gesticulation. Think of the two – intonation and gesticulation – as uniquely human paints that colour our speech. They make it more interesting for our listeners and readers, and help them focus on what we are saying.

 OVER TO YOU
A sentence starts with a capital letter and needs at least one punctuation mark. Three different punctuation marks can be placed at the end of a sentence (not all at once!). Do you know which ones?

DID YOU KNOW?

If you have ever heard that punctuation marks are used 'where we would pause during speaking or reading', that is not entirely correct.

Yes, **we do pause after full stops, question marks and exclamation marks** – they are all at the end of a sentence. When punctuation marks are inside sentences, it's a bit more complicated. So, for now, it's best to think of pausing mostly at the end of the sentence.

Are any punctuation marks more important than others? Some are certainly used more often than others. Imagine a pizza made of all the punctuation marks. What would be the biggest slice: full stops, colons, question marks, exclamations marks or commas?

If you said full stops, you're right. Most sentences have a full stop at the end.

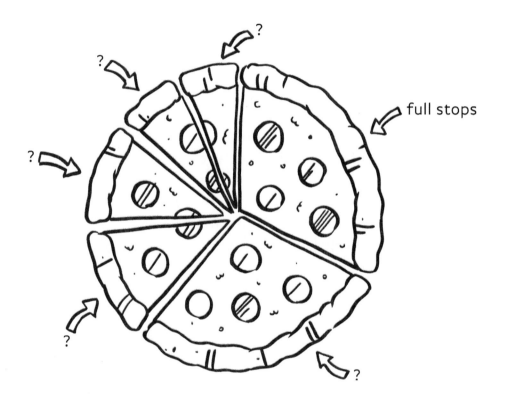

What's the second biggest slice? Check the chart below. Were you right?

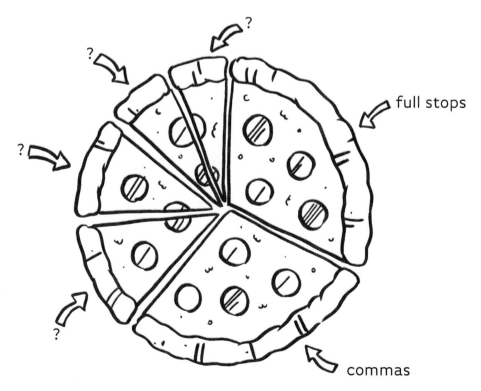

Now open any story book and count all the punctuation marks you can find on two random pages. If there are too many to count, estimate their numbers, then complete the pizza chart on the previous page. Check if your results are close to those in the Answer Key section at the back of the book.

2
Capital Letter

THINGS THAT CAPITAL LETTERS ARE NOT

✗ teachers' pet peeve

✗ rocket science

✗ punctuation marks

 STOP AND THINK
If capital letters are not punctuation marks, why should we be interested in them?

If you know how to end a sentence, you need to know how to start one, too.

The **FIRST WORD OF A SENTENCE** starts with a capital letter.

A customer returned to the optician's with a pair of glasses he had bought the previous day**. H**e complained that the glasses were useless**. T**he optician took the man outside and asked him to look up at the sky**. S**urprised, the customer looked into the sky**. H**urriedly, the optician asked the customer what he could see**. T**he man said, '**I** can see the sun,' to which the optician replied as loudly as she could, '**N**inety-three million miles and you're complaining**!**'

17

That was an easy read, wasn't it? I could almost hear your well-paced reading voice. Every full stop and capital letter served as navigation points to help you breathe normally and decide how to best use your voice.

A **PROPER NAME** starts with a capital letter.

'Proper' means correct. It also means unique, one that everyone recognises.

I HAVE A PROPER NAME

You certainly do, Zed. A proper name is one that refers to a particular person (or robot), place, event or institution. Zed, Emma Brown, Mr Spencer, Portugal, Manchester United and Easter are all proper names.

> Sometimes I wake up grumpy. Other times I let her sleep.

 STOP AND THINK
What's my pet's name?

I promise there is a hamster in the sentence above. Have you noticed anything unusual about the word 'grumpy'? We usually associate it with feeling grumpy. Here, it's a proper name and needs a capital letter.

Sometimes I wake up **G**rumpy. Other times I let her sleep**.**

 OVER TO YOU
How many missing capital letters can you find in the passage below? Use the box below to re-write it.

 Two mysterious people live in my house**:** somebody and nobody**.** Somebody did it and nobody knows who**.**

I SAY BE SOMEBODY NOBODY THOUGHT YOU COULD BE

 STOP AND THINK
Why do we sometimes start words like 'Mum', 'Dad', 'Nan', 'Granny' and 'Grandad' with a capital letter, but not always?

When we capitalise these words, we refer to a specific person or persons that we are, or someone is, related to. They then become proper names, or proper nouns. When we write 'dad' or 'mums', we are using common nouns. A dad is someone who is a father and mums are a group of mothers in general.

LEMON SQUEEZY
These sentences don't look right. Can you re-write them so that all proper names start with capital letters?

dad didn't want every tom, dick and harry using our front garden bench.

. . . .

rob slater is training for the winter olympics.

. . . .

the queen will deliver a speech at the house of lords.

. . . .

when in rome, do as the romans do.

. . . .

an englishman's home is his castle.

. . . .

year 6 mums and dads waited outside the national gallery in london.

. . . .

would you rather have a house in the big apple or silicon valley?

. . . .

if the mountain will not come to mahomet, mahomet must go to the mountain.

. . . .

liz chang, a panorama journalist, reported live from westminster.

. . . .

please, two more minutes, dad. i'm not ready yet.

. . . .

if cinderella's shoe fit perfectly, then why did it fall off?

. . . .

STOP AND CHECK
Did you start all your sentences with a capital letter?

STEP IT UP
What play on words makes these jokes funny? If someone didn't get them, what clues would you give them?

My brother bought two goldfish and named them One and Two.
If one dies, he'll still have two.

. . . .

. . . .

"Can I have a bookmark?"
"My name is Mick."

. . . .

. . . .

I named my dog Five Miles so I can tell people that I walk five miles every day.

. . . .

. . . .

I see no end, have no control and no home anymore.
I think it's time for a new keyboard.

. . . .

. . . .

I used to be in a band called Lost Dog.
You probably saw our posters.

. . . .

. . . .

I WRITE ALL MY JOKES IN CAPITALS.
THIS ONE WAS WRITTEN IN BERLIN.

. . . .

. . . .

The name of **A DAY OR A MONTH** starts with a capital letter.

Can we invent a day between **S**aturday and **S**unday, please**?**
Of course**.** When two **S**undays come together**!**

April showers bring **M**ay flowers**.**

I KNOW A HUMAN AS MAD AS A MARCH HARE

Thank you for your compliment, Zed.

 STOP AND CHECK
Is that a **m**arch or **M**arch hare?

BREEZE THROUGH
This should be easy. Can you re-write the sentences so that all days of the week or month start with capital letters?

if mondays were shoes, they wouldn't walk very far.

. . . .

mrs ford always says tuesday is just monday's ugly sister.

. . . .

can february march? no, but april may.

. . . .

why are solders tired in april? they've had a long march.

. . . .

did you know that may is the shortest month? it only has three letters.

. . . .

thirty days has september, april, june and november...

. . . .

THIRTY DAYS HAS SEPTEMBER ALL THE REST I CANT REMEMBER

 STOP AND CHECK
Did you start all your sentences with a capital letter?

23

The name of **A LANGUAGE** starts with a capital letter.

My Mum can say 'No' in **E**nglish, **F**rench, **I**talian and **S**panish**!**

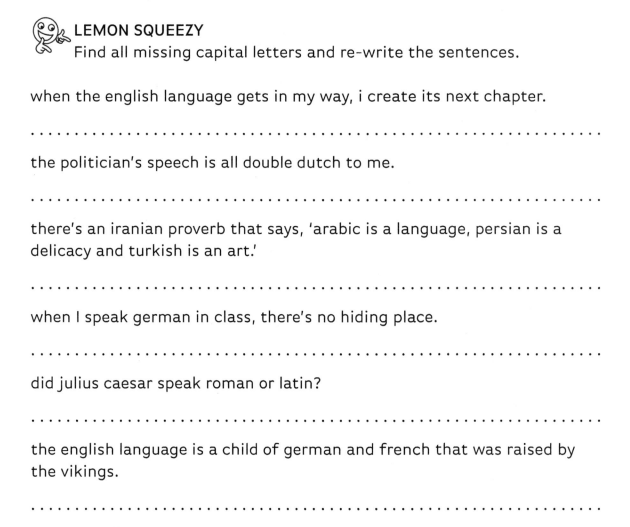

LEMON SQUEEZY
Find all missing capital letters and re-write the sentences.

when the english language gets in my way, i create its next chapter.

. . . .

the politician's speech is all double dutch to me.

. . . .

there's an iranian proverb that says, 'arabic is a language, persian is a delicacy and turkish is an art.'

. . . .

when I speak german in class, there's no hiding place.

. . . .

did julius caesar speak roman or latin?

. . . .

the english language is a child of german and french that was raised by the vikings.

. . . .

 STOP AND CHECK
Did you start all your sentences with a capital letter?

CAPITAL LETTER

A word expressing a **CONNOTATION WITH A PLACE** starts with a capital letter.

Do you fancy **I**ndian or **C**hinese for dinner**?**

Mum walked through the **F**rench doors with a tray of **V**iennese biscuits**.**

 OVER TO YOU
Find all missing capital letters and re-write the sentences.

we asked the hairdresser whether it's called the french plait or french braid.

. . . .

the class played chinese whispers all morning.

. . . .

scientists believe the western world plays russian roulette with antibiotics.

. . . .

autumn heatwaves are called indian summers.

. . . .

we always have peking duck and cantonese soup in this restaurant.

. . . .

every time we shop for furniture, we end up having swedish meatballs.

. . . .

i'd love to know how the earth rotates; it would surely make my day.

. . . .

STOP AND CHECK
Did you start all your sentences with a capital letter?

The name of **A NATIONALITY OR AN ETHNIC GROUP** starts with a capital letter.

> What the **B**ritish people call crisps, the **A**mericans call chips.
> What the **B**ritish call chips, the **A**mericans call **F**rench fries.

I WAS MADE IN CHINA SO A PART OF ME IS CHINESE

STEP IT UP

How's your knowledge of geography? Find all missing capital letters, then re-write the sentences in full.

A group of northern european countries that includes denmark, norway and sweden is called . . . .

The people who live there are. . . . .

. . . .

. . . .

. . . .

Some people think that poland is in eastern europe; others believe that it's part of central europe. That makes the poles either . . . .

. . . . or . . . .

. . . .

. . . .

. . . .

The ethnic group of americans whose ancestors came from africa are called

. . . .

. . . .

. . . .

Mexico, central america and most of south america where spanish is the primary language were once under spanish rule. Their cultures are referred

to as . . . . cultures.

. . . .

. . . .

. . . .

The name of **A HISTORICAL PERIOD** starts with a capital letter.

> My time machine took me to the **M**iddle **A**ges and the **I**ndustrial **R**evolution, where I briefly met **D**octor **W**ho.

 LEMON SQUEEZY
How's your knowledge of historical jokes? Find all missing capital letters and re-write the jokes.

Q: Why were the early days of history called the dark ages?
A: Because there were so many knights!

. . . .

. . . .

Q: How was the roman empire cut in half?
A: With a pair of caesars!

. . . .

. . . .

Q: How did the vikings send secret messages?
A: By norse code!

. . . .

. . . .

Q: What comes after the bronze age and the iron age?
A: The heavy metal age, Sir.

. . . .

. . . .

Q: Where did the medieval king john sign the magna carta?
A: At the bottom.

. . . .

. . . .

The name of **A HOLIDAY OR A HOLY DAY** starts with a capital letter.

Chinese **N**ew **Y**ear, **E**aster, **D**iwali, **H**anukkah and **C**hristmas are all our favourite times of the year.

 STEP IT UP
How's your knowledge of religious festivals? Find all missing capital letters and complete each passage.

The festival of lights and the feast of dedication are two other names for a jewish holiday that is observed for eight days and nights, and is called

. . . .

Hanging stockings out comes from the dutch custom of leaving shoes packed with food for st nicholas's donkeys. St nicholas would leave small gifts in return. This religious festival is called . . . .

. . . . is an important religious festival in india celebrated between october and november. People often think of it as a hindu festival, but it is also celebrated by sikhs and jains.

. . . . new year starts a new animal's zodiac year. In china, each lunar cycle has 60 years and 12 years is regarded as a small cycle. Each of the 12 years is defined by an animal sign. 2020 is the year of the rat and 2021 is the year of the ox.

. . . ., a christian holiday, celebrates the resurrection of jesus christ. During holy week, holy thursday commemorates when the last supper was held. Good friday commemorates jesus's crucifixion and death.

During . . . ., which lasts a month, muslims don't eat or drink between dawn and sunset. Fasting helps them devote themselves to their faith and get closer to allah. It is one of the five pillars of islam, which form the basis of how muslims live their lives.

The word 'carol' means dance or song of praise and joy. Carols used to be sung during all four seasons, but the tradition of singing them at . . . . is the only one to survive.

The first word, and each significant word, of a **TITLE** starts with a capital letter.

If I could take only one thing to a desert island, it would be a copy of **'H**ow to **B**uild a **B**oat**'**.

OR HOW TO BUILD A ROBOT BY CY BORG

How would a robot help on a desert island?

HAVENT YOU READ THE BOOK BY PETER BROWN

I forgot about 'The Wild Robot'. Thanks, Zed.

BREEZE THROUGH

This part is all about you! Don't forget capital letters when writing down titles.

The computer game I've played the most times is _____.

The only time you'll see a fight over the remote control in my house is when _____ is on.

The movie I've watched the most times is _____ _____.

The book I would like to author one day would be called _____ _____.

The book I would give to my best friend is _____ _____ by _____.

The book I would give to my teacher is _____ _____ by _____.

Newspapers and magazines you are likely to find in my house are _____.

My favourite TV programme is _____ _____.

My least favourite TV programme is _____ _____ .

The songs I like to listen to at the moment are _____ _____.

My favourite comedy programme is _____ _____.

The first word of a **DIRECT QUOTATION THAT IS A SENTENCE** starts with a capital letter.

When I got my first bike, my mother said, **'It**'s not the falling off that hurts, it's the landing**.'**

DOGS WITH WET NOSES HURT MORE THAN BAD LANDING

Do they tickle you?

THEY INTERFERE WITH MY ELECTRIC CIRCUITS

Shocking!

TAKE A BOW
What would others say? Stories with unexpected twists and turns can be very exciting. In this one, you are reporting what you and others said (or what they would have said if they could talk). Don't forget to start every quotation (what was said, word for word) with a capital letter.

It all happened so quickly. I simply said, **'M**y homework can wait.**'**

Mum stopped typing and asked, **'W**ould you like some help?**'**

In my mind's eye, I saw Jack Sparrow wink at me and shout,

'. . . . .!**'**

At that moment, the movie stopped playing, but my PlayStation made a whirring noise, which to me sounded like a perfect question,

'. . . . .?**'**

To my left, Harry Potter's face on my pencil case whispered,

'. . . . .**'**

Just then my phone rang, and my best friend yelled,

'. . . . .!**'**

I hope that's what he said because I was distracted by my sister's dance shoes marching out of the shoe cupboard and crying,

'. . . . .**'**

Luckily, Dad walked in and restored order by announcing,

'. . . . .**'**

I swear I could hear the Prime Minister on Dad's newspaper front cry out,

'. . . . .**'**

I immediately thought of my old teacher, who used to say,

'. . . . .**'**

Then Yoda looked down from my 'Star Wars' poster and pronounced,

'..'

I'm not a Jedi, but I thought it was polite to reply to Yoda, so I said,

'..'

In the end, the only thing I could possibly say to Mum was,

'..'

STOP AND CHECK
Did you start all direct quotations with a capital letter?

A **BRAND NAME** starts with a capital letter.

It's silly to give cats **K**ellogg's cereals, unless it's **M**ice **K**rispies.

IS STAR WARS A TITLE OR A BRAND NAME ASKING FOR R2-D2

LEMON SQUEEZY
Check for all missing capital letters, then re-write the sentences in full.

i just got hit on the head with a power tool. i was sitting there minding my own business, the next thing I know, bosch!

. . . .

. . . .

samsung, iPhone or motorola – i can't picture myself without a camera phone.

. . . .

. . . .

honestly, ice hockey is just a bunch of people fighting for the last oreo.

. . . .

. . . .

if apple built a house, would it have windows?

. . . .

. . . .

i just stepped on some cheerios on the floor. you can call me a cereal killer!

. . . .

. . . .

why did the yellow m&m go to school?
because it wanted to be a smartie.

. . . .

. . . .

there's a new a travel guide highlighting towns and cities with badly laid paving slabs. it's called tripadvisor!

. . . .

. . . .

i thought i'd use my tesco clubcard to scrape the ice off my windscreen, but I could only get 10% off.

. . . .

. . . .

BREEZE THROUGH
Here's your quick-fire quiz. Write the first thing that comes to your mind. Don't forget capital letters.

QUICK-FIRE QUIZ

No cheating. You have 10 seconds for each line.
Write down the name of **one**:

online search engine: _____

online store: _____

company from a TV advert: _____

jeans brand: _____

vlogging service: _____

electronics brand (TVs, mobile phones): _____

fashion brand: _____

high street store: _____

cinema chain: _____

supermarket: _____

coffee shop: _____

airline: _____

sweet/chocolate brand: _____

Did you get 7 or more? You rock!
Did you start all brand names with capital letters?

ABBREVIATIONS and **ROMAN NUMERALS** are all capital letters.

The **BBC** stands for **B**ritish **B**roadcasting **C**orporation.

STEP IT UP
Can you write out these abbreviations in full?

ICT ....

AKA ....

DIY ....

FAQ ....

ETA ....

BAFTA ....

RSVP ....

DOB ....

RSPCA ....

NATO ....

LGBT ....

PTO ....

NHS ....

> **MMXIX** is 2019, **MMXX** is 2020, and **MMXXIII** is...?

> **I** struggle with **R**oman numerals until I get to 159, then it **CLIX.**
>
> Is **LXXX** love and kisses**?** Or 80**?**

 TAKE A BOW

These Roman numerals are also short words and abbreviations. But what's their Arabic numeral value? Connect the pairs that go together.

I	200
MIX	600
CC	1
CD	1100
CV	400
DC	1009
MC	54
MD	105
LIV	501
DI	1500

THE PRONOUN I is always a capital letter.

If **I** am nobody and nobody is perfect – **I** am perfect.

OVER TO YOU

Write a story that is six sentences long, in which the pronoun I is used at least 10 times in total.

··

··

··

··

··

··

··

··

··

··

··

··

··

3

Full Stop

Someone's got a lot of homework to do. Poor Jack hasn't got very far with his work.

That's all I've finished.

 STOP AND THINK
Where could we place an extra full stop in the sentence above to help Jack finish his work?

That's all. I've finished.

Jack is not simply pleased, he is shouting out his joy to the rest of the world! An exclamation mark at the end of the sentence might fit even better.

That's all. I've finished!

The full stop split two separate ideas:

1. there's nothing else left to do ('That's all')

and

2. I'm free to go now ('I've finished!')

That was easy.

I'm sorry. You can't go to the sleepover!

 STOP AND THINK
Is there anything we can do to make Alfie's Mum less cross?

We can remove the exclamation mark and replace it with a full stop. Now Alfie's Mum's voice seems far less angry. But what can we do with the full stop after 'I'm sorry'? Replace it? With what? Remove it? Let's try taking it out.

I'm sorry you can't go to the sleepover.

Aww... I can hear Mum's soft voice. Perhaps Alfie hasn't been naughty after all but unwell, or the sleepover has been cancelled. One thing we know for certain is that a change in our use of punctuation can alter a story quite dramatically.

When you read the sentence the first time, the full stop after 'I'm sorry' made you pause, which gave you enough time to adjust your voice to sound cross and maybe disappointed. In this way, the full stop made you feel the story. It sent a message to your brain to read with different intonation and a louder voice.

CROSS AND DISAPPOINTED ARE NEGATIVE EMOTIONS

You are just a narrator, Zed. And narrators, as well as actors, are not *really* angry or disappointed.

KEY TAKEAWAY

A full stop is at the end of a sentence to show that it is finished.

Full stops tell us to pause between sentences.

They make thoughts and ideas more complete.

They also give writing more structure (show the way sentences should be built).

BREEZE THROUGH

Let's start with something easy to warm you up. Can you put in all missing full stops and capital letters?

everything is funnier when you are not allowed to laugh

· ·

· ·

my first name is joe my surname is brown

· ·

· ·

it's easier to pull than to push it's also easier to sit than to stand

· ·

· ·

every class has one really funny student

· ·

· ·

dan bought chicken and eastern spice he is a fan of moroccan kebabs

· ·

· ·

i am told i am too cool for school

. . . .

. . . .

chocolate is god's apology for broccoli

. . . .

. . . .

i didn't know ankara was the capital of turkey

. . . .

. . . .

 STEP IT UP
These pairs of sentences are punctuated differently depending on their meaning. Can you add missing full stops? Don't forget to start each new sentence with a capital letter.

it's not true he wrote the letter (*He didn't write the letter.*)

. . . .

. . . .

it's not true he wrote the letter (*The truth is that he wrote the letter.*)

. . . .

. . . .

easy does it

. . . .

that was easy does it mean I can do it myself from now on?

. . . .

. . . .

it was true love

. . . .

it was true love struck Ahmed at the very moment he looked at Rabia

. . . .

. . . .

we are trying to speak perfect French

. . . .

we are trying to speak perfect French is to learn to roll your 'r's

. . . .

. . . .

i don't know Katie (*I don't know the girl called Katie.*)

. . . .

. . . .

i don't know Katie might (*Katie might know the answer.*)

. . . .

. . . .

we are friends forever

. . . .

we are friends forever seems shorter now

. . . .

. . . .

I WILL FULL STOP AT NOTHING

I know, Zed. Be patient. Your punctuation software should arrive any day. Imagine reading all stories without changing their meaning!

 OVER TO YOU
Full stops separate complete ideas. Could you write correct sentences (with full stops and capital letters) in the boxes? Then draw simple illustrations to show what each idea is about. The first set has been done for you.

sorry i'm late i didn't want to come

Sorry I'm late.

I didn't want to come.

ryan took a ruler to bed he was upset it didn't say how long he slept

cinderella didn't make it to the football team she ran away from the ball

dad's job is super confidential he really hasn't got a clue what he's doing

some people say i'm lazy i say i'm on energy saving mode

love is in the air i'm going to wear my gas mask

fruit is 90% water it is also 100% not pizza

my teacher asked me to name all chemicals in the periodic table i thought they already had names

my teacher asked me to name all chemicals in the periodic table i thought they already had names

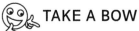 **TAKE A BOW**

Jay wrote a sci-fi story with the help of his cat Gremlin. Can you help Jay put in all missing full stops and capital letters? Gremlin says, 'Use a pencil and thank me later.'

I decided to clone myself I thought I could send my clone to school while I stayed at home and played computer games it obviously had to be a secret I swore my cat Gremlin not to utter a single meow to anyone I saw Dr Frankenbrain in the school lab and explained I needed to finish my old chemistry project he let Gremlin be my guinea pig so long as he behaved himself all was going well until Gremlin spotted a red dot on the cloning machine's controls and went mad chasing the light as well as its reflection on the wall Dr Frankenbrain jumped in to help me manage the silly cat the move was a disaster as the place was full of fragile instruments and dangerous equipment what I didn't know was that my teacher was really clumsy he tripped over a cable and got zapped by the revving machine although he didn't get cloned he became one fortieth of his normal size he was much smaller than Gremlin I asked Dr Frankenbrain what I should do to get him back to his normal size all I got back was a series of high-pitched squeaks Gremlin the mad mice chaser did not wait for an invitation he pounced on Dr Frankenbrain and ate him up in three superfast gulps a shame really because I couldn't think of anyone else who could help me clone myself as I was tidying up the lab Gremlin gave out the loudest burp I've ever heard which actually turned out to be my teacher's real voice...

4

Exclamation Mark

What do you call someone who loves animals? Bhavna. Bhavna loves all animals equally and... Wait, what is that noise?

> Help! A bear!

 STOP AND THINK
What makes us change our intonation when reading this sentence?

If Bhavna sounds overly dramatic, it's because of the two exclamation marks. They literally make the narrator raise their eyebrows and cry out in a loud, high-pitched voice.

We've got to help Bhavna. We can start by taking out one of the exclamation marks.

Help a bear**!**

Although Bhavna is not in danger anymore, she needs you to support her charity. Her message is loud and clear with the final exclamation mark.

DID YOU KNOW?

The name 'exclamation mark' comes from the Latin word 'Io', which meant 'Hurray'.

Io = Hurray

In time, the 'I' gradually moved on top of the 'o' and became the punctuation mark we use today.

KEY TAKEAWAY

An exclamation mark is at the end of a sentence that expresses a lot of feeling, for example enthusiasm, certainty and anger. It is also used to give an order or instruction.

Remember not to use two or three exclamation marks in a row (!!!), unless it's a personal message or letter.

Do not leave a gap between a word and an exclamation mark:

Excellent ! Instead write: Excellent!

LEMON SQUEEZY
Can you put in missing punctuation marks? Check that all sentences start with a capital letter.

that mini heart attack you get when your foot slides down the stairs

. . . .

stop talking and listen

. . . .

i'm so glad i don't have to take this test again

. . . .

go don't look back go

. . . .

my sister asked me to pass her the chapstick, but I accidentally passed her a glue stick she still hasn't spoken to me

. . . .

. . . .

i can cut down a tree only using my vision it's true i saw it with my
own eyes

. . . .

three conspiracy theorists walk into a bar you can't tell me that's just
a coincidence

. . . .

. . . .

so what if I don't know what apocalypse means it's not the end of the world

. . . .

. . . .

BREEZE THROUGH
A full stop or an exclamation mark? Add correct punctuation marks at the end of each sentence and check for missing capital letters.

Stop you're ruining my new coat

Maybe now is not the best time

The seat is mine get over it

I don't know why i couldn't sleep last night

How exciting i didn't know mr brantley is getting married

Wow i simply love it

It's a really lovely meal thank you

He's just won the lottery you don't say

Come back now

I still think getting ann a game was a better idea than a pack of socks

Unbelievable the dress was £100

I can see a spider quick get it out of my bedroom

Don't bite my arm off it's only a joke

It's very peaceful on this side of the hill

You've managed to do it all in under an hour that's amazing

5

Question Mark

A picture is worth a thousand words, which is roughly the length of a typical PowerPoint presentation to Year 7 students.

Homework never killed a child, but why should I take a chance?

What if my brain steams up and my ears burn**?**
What if my eyes go red and I can't read anymore**?**
Do you really want to feel like you're a bad parent**?**
Why would I tell you that Buster had eaten my homework**?**
Would I risk the poor dog's life, too**?**
Where am I going**?** Do I need permission to leave the room**?**
What's wrong with going to lie down**?**
Please, can we stop mentioning homework now**?**

Homework never killed a child, but why should I take a chance**?**

I think Ella's presentation to her Dad is rather convincing, don't you?

WHY ONLY QUESTIONS

That was the idea, Zed. In this homework, students were only allowed to use sentences with question marks. It must've been quite hard. But it looks like a good homework to me.

NO QUESTION MARKS IN MY PROGRAMING LANGUAGE

Your manual says that you understand 'variables', such as IF, ELSE, FOR and WHILE. But don't worry, I'm working on your missing punctuation so you can appreciate the human language.

I DONT LIKE HOMEWORK WITH QUESTION MARKS

Well, Dad liked it. He smiled a few times and laughed out loud twice. He said, 'Plotting with a child never killed a parent, but why should I take a chance?'

GOOD ON DAD

DID YOU KNOW?

Legend has it that, in ancient Egypt, the question mark took its shape from a cat's tail. Sadly, there are no records of ancient Egyptians using punctuation marks at all, even though they were very keen on cats!

What we can be more certain of is that, in the Middle Ages, the word 'question' was abbreviated to 'qo', which, just as was the case with the exclamation mark, gradually changed its shape when 'q' moved on top of the 'o'.

qo = question

q
o   became   **?**

KEY TAKEAWAY

A question mark is at the end of a sentence asking a question.

Never leave a gap between a word and a question mark:

Really **?**   Instead write: Really**?**

LEMON SQUEEZY

These jokes and punchy one-liners will make more sense when all punctuation marks are there. Can you insert the missing question marks, exclamation marks, full stops and capital letters?

Would you mind helping me out
Of course which way did you come in

. . . .

. . . .

What do you call security guards outside the samsung shop
Guardians of the galaxy

. . . .

. . . .

Knock, knock
Who's there
Little old lady
Little old lady who
I didn't know you could yodel

. . . .

. . . .

. . . .

. . . .

. . . .

Did you hear about the new reversible jackets
I'm excited to see how they turn out

. . . .

. . . .

Who is the laziest person on earth
Whoever named the fireplace

. . . .

. . . .

Did you hear about the little girl who went upstairs to get some medicine
I think she's coming down with something

. . . .

. . . .

Why is the human brain amazing
It works as soon as you wake up and it doesn't stop until you get to school

. . . .

. . . .

Change is hard
Have you ever managed to bend a coin

. . . .

. . . .

Mr morris, why are maths books sad
I don't know, alfie. Why are they sad
Because they have problems to solve

. . . .

. . . .

. . . .

Did you hear about the kidnapping at school
It's okay he woke up

. . . .

. . . .

Isn't it scary that doctors call what they do 'practice'

. . . .

Pencils could be made with erasers at both ends, but what would be
the point

. . . .

What do you call blueberries playing the guitar
A jam session

. . . .

. . . .

How many months of the year have 28 days
All of them

. . . .

. . . .

What time is it when 10 elephants are chasing you
Ten to one

. . . .

. . . .

Did you hear about the hungry clock
It went back four seconds

. . . .

. . . .

Why is 'abbreviation' such a long word

. . . .

Wouldn't exercise be more fun if calories screamed while you burned them

. . . .

Don't you hate it when someone answers their own questions
I do

. . . .

. . . .

Why do seagulls fly over the sea
Because if they flew over the bay they'd be bagels

. . . .

. . . .

Why do adults ask children what they want to be when they grow up
They're looking for ideas

. . . .

. . . .

Am i ambivalent well, yes and no

. . . .

The teacher said 'Name two pronouns'
I said, 'Who Me'

. . . .

. . . .

What's the difference between a good joke and a bad joke timing

. . . .

. . . .

Why do people believe you when you say there are four billion stars, but
check when you say the paint is wet

. . . .

. . . .

Why didn't noah swat those two mosquitos

. . . .

Isn't it amazing that the amount of news that happens around the world every day always exactly fits the newspaper

. . . .

. . . .

Why do banks have their doors open but chain the pens to the counters

. . . .

. . . .

What if there were no rhetorical questions

. . . .

6

Listing Comma

There once lived a girl called Ying who loved cooking, her family and her cats. Everyone liked Ying.

I love cooking, my family and my cats.

When Ying rushed her writing, her teacher was alarmed to read what she loved the most.

I love cooking my family and my cats.

STOP AND THINK
What's the secret behind Ying's terrifying alter ego?

The secret is that there's no secret. There's only a comma missing in Ying's writing.

SHE IS A MONSTER

Is she, Zed? It is punctuation (or rather the lack of it) that changed Ying's tale into a horror story.

Next time you wonder if it really matters that we use commas, picture Ying's wooden spoon ready to stir inside the tall steaming pot. The spoon is so heavy that Ying might need both hands to push the cat's tail back into the pot. See a tiny bone pop up and...

I CANT SEE ANY COMMAS IN THE POT

Thank you for spoiling my analogy, Zed.

DID YOU KNOW?

The name 'comma' comes from the Greek word 'komma'.

komma = something cut off

The comma separates (cuts off) items that we are listing in the sentence. It also 'cuts off' separate parts of the sentence (clauses) – more about that in later chapters.

Do we pause after a comma? Yes, slightly.

Should we put a comma where we feel we'd pause when speaking? Not always, so don't use this rule in writing.

 OVER TO YOU
Ying's friend Mona is a pretty fast runner. Or should I write 'pretty, fast runner'? Can you match the pictures to the correct sentences?

1. She's a pretty, fast girl.
2. She's a pretty fast girl.

 STOP AND THINK
How do we know when to put a comma between two adjectives (words that describe someone or something)?

If we can replace the comma with 'and', then we're listing things (pretty and fast). **Listing = comma.**

If we can't replace the comma with 'and', we are not listing anything (pretty fast). Here we are simply describing how fast the girl is – in this case, she is pretty fast. It doesn't matter if she is pretty or not.

Do I need to add that anyone who focuses on people's looks before anything else is pretty shallow?

Commas separate things or people in a list.

Let's play rock, paper **and** scissors.

I like Tom, Khalid, Maduo **and** Orla.

Commas don't just separate single words.

The ideal student doesn't forget homework, doesn't day-dream, doesn't look outside the classroom window, doesn't shout, doesn't run in the corridor, doesn't make a mess, doesn't upset other students **and** doesn't exist.

Later in the book, you'll find out that it's also possible to use semicolons, not only commas, to separate more 'wordy' chunks inside a text (or check the *Semicolon* section now).

There is no comma between the last two things in a list because 'and' separates them.

> ...paper **and** scissors**.**
>
> ...doesn't upset other students **and** doesn't exist**.**

You might say that 'and' replaces the last comma. This way the reader knows there are no more items in the list.

KEY TAKEAWAY

Commas separate things or people in a list. They also separate phrases within longer sentences.

We do not put a comma where we feel we'd pause when speaking. This rule is not a reliable one.

LEMON SQUEEZY
Can you put in all missing listing commas and full stops?

Chaos panic upset shock and disorder – my work here is done

Time doesn't exist but wrist watches pocket watches kinetic watches digital watches analogue watches wall clocks Grandpa clocks and all other clocks do

Remember you are unique one-of-a-kind original and completely incomparable – just like everyone else

Advice for those who don't succeed the first time: stop right there redefine 'success' redefine 'at first' and destroy all evidence that you've tried

If you make friends with someone lend them money watch them walk away and never see them again – the money was worth it

I went to Ikea hid in a wardrobe waited for the first person to open it and shouted out 'Welcome to Narnia!'

So far I've visited Birmingham Manchester Leeds Liverpool and York

We've seen all zoo animals apart from pandas lemurs otters tamarins and elephants

We had to calculate the cost of four cups of coffee and three cups of tea check if £15 was enough to pay for all the drinks work out the ratio between coffee and tea purchased convert it into a percentage figure show the findings in a diagram and report to the teacher

Daisy's to-do list included tidying shelves and cupboards writing a message to Mia starting a geography homework calling Grandad in Newport and browsing Amazon for a new pencil case

7

Serial (Oxford) Comma

Sometimes we need a comma before 'and' to avoid a very specific type of confusion. That comma is then called the serial comma, or the Oxford comma.

I love my parents, Ed Sheeran, **and** Lady Gaga.

 STOP AND THINK
The comma before 'and' looks odd. Should it be there?

Let's see what will happen if we take it out.

I love my parents, Ed Sheeran and Lady Gaga.

Now it looks like Ed Sheeran and Lady Gaga are Daisy's parents. Their names are side by side between the comma and the full stop. But adding the extra comma separates them as different people that Daisy loves.

NOBODY TOLD ME LADY GAGA AND ED SHEERAN HAD A CHILD

For a good reason, Zed – because it never happened! Did you even listen? Remind me to get an engineer over to check your processor again.

MY NAME IS ZED NOT ALEXA

WHAT'S THE FUSS ABOUT THE SERIAL COMMA?

We don't use the serial comma very often. When we do, it's when it's likely to change the meaning of a sentence. Legal documents and research papers use the serial comma because in these documents there is no room for any misunderstanding.

You are not advised to use it in school writing unless you are really sure why you use it. And if you see a comma in an unexpected place in a book, it's most probable that the writer is avoiding confusion (ambiguity is another good word for confusion).

KEY TAKEAWAY

The serial (or Oxford) comma is placed after the last but one item in a list of three or more items, before 'and' or 'or'.

Its role is to add clarity to a potentially confusing sentence.

STEP IT UP

Can you put in all missing punctuation marks, including listing and serial commas?

The best fruit are peaches apples wild strawberries and blueberries

My brother is free at the weekend Monday and Wednesday (*he will be working on Tuesday, Thursday and Friday*)

Please may I order today's special deal cheese and biscuits (*cheese and biscuits are two separate items*)

Please may I order today's special deal cheese and biscuits (*cheese and biscuits is today's special deal*)

We can't decorate your bedroom without new paint dustsheets paintbrushes and a ladder

My historical heroes are the Romans Julius Caesar and Augustus

My historical heroes are the Romans Nelson and Churchill

Please could we have two cheeseburgers one bag of fish fingers three packets of crisps and three glasses of water

Don't forget to collect cat food milk flour and raspberry jam

Harriet missed history design technology and geography lessons because her bus broke down

Who doesn't like the Queen's corgis William and Kate

8

Name-Separating Comma

You know, Zed? As much as I enjoy having you as my assistant...

Actually because I got used to you. You sometimes remind me of a parrot that could talk but didn't understand commas. Some very unexpected things happened, let me tell you.

The parrot was called Wendy and she was a royal gift to Captain Fitzpatrick. One evening, the captain rolled his 'r's particularly dramatically: 'Pirrrates on boarrrd!' The well-meaning parrot took no time to announce, 'Let's fight, Captain Fitzpatrick!'

Let's fight,
Captain
Fitzpatrick!

Unfortunately, what was heard was:

Let's fight
Captain
Fitzpatrick**!**

 STOP AND THINK
How did a single comma change the captain's fate?

The comma added clarity to Wendy's advice about who she was referring to. When we refer to a specific person (or animal and even a thing) in our writing, separating their name makes it clear what we mean.

HUMANS SAY ONE THING AND MEAN A TROUBLE

'Another', not 'a trouble', Zed.

I KNOW TROUBLE WHEN I HEAR ONE

If the Captain Fitzpatrick's story is not enough of a cautionary tale, look no further than the next example. All that is left for me to say is, 'Keep the children safe with a comma.'

Time to eat children.

Time to eat, children.

THE WOLF HAS SHRUNK THE CHILDREN

Or the children are little and very scared, Zed.

KEY TAKEAWAY

A comma separates names in a sentence so that the reader is clear who the writer is referring to.

Without this function, the meaning of some sentences may be lost.

 OVER TO YOU
Can you match the pictures to the correct sentences?

A

B

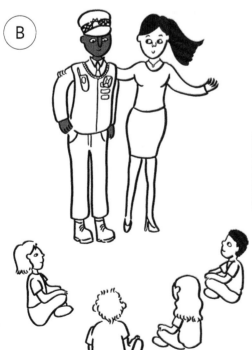

1. Phil the policeman is here.
2. Phil, the policeman is here.

C

3. Call him Jack and see if he answers.

4. Call him, Jack, and see if he answers.

D

E

5. If you like Zoya, I'll leave you.
6. If you like, Zoya, I'll leave you.

F

7. It's raining cats and dogs.

8. It's raining, cats and dogs.

TAKE A BOW
Can you draw simple cartoons to go with these captions?

I'm going bananas.

I'm going, bananas.

I don't know, London.

I don't know London.

We are sitting ducks.

We are sitting, ducks.

9

Clause the Santa Claus

It makes perfect sense to think that sentences are made of words, but actually it is clauses, not words, that are the building blocks of sentences. If we were allowed to string words together any way we liked, then words would be our building blocks. But in English, as in any other language, that would create serious communication problems.

World information there supermarket up and the I went many asked in how to the desk supermarkets are.

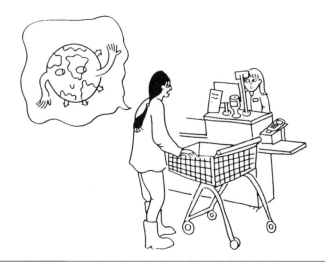

I went up to the supermarket information desk and asked how many supermarkets there are in the world.

That's better!

To avoid confusion, we have rules that tell us **in what order** words are put together. These rules are part of a system called syntax.

You can think of clauses as sets of ready-made building block structures. Imagine how much faster you could build a toy airplane if some parts had been assembled for you. Once you've taken out one part from a box, say a ready-made cockpit, you feel more confident that you're building the right model.

Clauses are the separate parts that you put together to produce a grammatically correct sentence.

CLAWS IS

Clauses, Zed. Groups of words that go together in a sentence. There may be one or more clauses in a single sentence. Each clause needs a head, you know... someone in charge.

ROBOTS ARE GOOD HEADS THEY SOLVE PROBLEMS FASTER

Yes, but robots are not as flexible as humans. You're still learning to use full stops after countless reboots. I'm not sure you'd be good being left in charge just yet. But stop distracting me, Zed. I wanted to say that **a verb** is the head in every clause.

THE DOING WORD

Exactly. Words like 'go' and 'went', and word combinations like 'have gone', 'is going', 'should've gone' are all in charge in clauses. They give each clause a distinctive meaning.

Look at this example:

When school is over, we run home through the park.

There are two clauses in this sentence. Each has a different message specified by the verb:

1. school **is** over

and

2. we **run** home through the park

There are sentences with as many as three or more clauses. Look at this one:

Just as I picked up the pen, it started doodling instead of writing, which made Sonya giggle.

We have three clauses because there are three separate ideas in the sentence:

1. I **picked up** the pen

2. the pen **started** doodling instead of writing

3. this **made** Sonya giggle

CLAUSE SOUNDS LIKE SANTA CLAUS

You're not wrong, although the clause we are interested in has an 'e' at the end.

Before I became Santa Claus, I was Claus.

+ **e** = claus**e**

You've just given me an idea, Zed. If I draw Santa's head before each clause, you'll learn to recognise them much faster.

 When school is over, we run home through the park.

 Just as I picked up the pen, it started doodling instead of writing, which made Sonya giggle.

KEY TAKEAWAY

A clause is a part of a sentence.

Sentences are made of clauses, which are often described as the building blocks of sentences.

Each clause's head (main part) is a verb (or words acting as verbs). It's not possible to have a clause without a verb in it.

OVER TO YOU

Santa or not? Decide which groups of words taken out of sentences are clauses, and which are not. Look for verbs (doing words). Draw Santa heads next to all clauses.

✗ _____ In a nutshell.

🎅 _____ but that **would make** no sense at all!

_____ a long, windy road to my village.

_____ He wasn't argumentative.

_____ which went down rather well.

_____ It must've been very frightening for Johnny,

_____ I immediately thought of you.

_____ No more for me.

_____ Unless you ask,

_____ In reality,

_____ Putting the issues aside,

_____ Promptly,

_____ Wasn't it just?

_____ You are welcome.

_____ At the top of the stairs,

_____ Sit down, Pudding!

_____ However,

_____ Michael,

_____ which surprised me.

STEP IT UP

How many clauses are there in each sentence? Start by finding words that act as clause heads.

3 When I **was** a child, my family **moved** a lot, but I always **found** them.

_____ Take my advice – I'm not using it.

_____ If there is a wrong way to do something, someone will do it.

_____ Don't mention it, honestly.

_____ Whether Syd did it, or Mel made him do it, we will never know.

_____ The dog, which was left behind the locked gate, barked furiously.

_____ Living on Earth is expensive, but it does include a free trip around the Sun.

_____ Unbelievably, Paula was described as a happy-go-lucky girl.

_____ Ted, who is only ten years old, has the making of a great chef.

_____ She told them that I didn't know what I wanted for Christmas.

_____ Sienna shouted that she had already been to that theme park.

_____ The author, who was late to the book signing event, couldn't read the first chapter because he'd forgotten his glasses.

_____ I was raised as an only child, which really annoyed my siblings.

_____ Dad hit the brake, which caused the car to swerve.

_____ In all honesty, I haven't met a nicer couple than Jed and Jo.

_____ I laughed because the joke she had told us had the wrong ending.

_____ If you tell Nan, I'll tell Grandad, and we'll both be in trouble.

_____ When your only tool is a hammer, all your problems look like nails.

10
Comma Separating Clauses

Jack loves all sports. The most competitive student at school, he has to win every game and every race. Until yesterday, no one could challenge Jack in athletics. But today Sheng has joined Jack's class. Both boys are very fast runners, but who is faster: Jack or Sheng?

1. Jack chased Sheng shouting **'I'm faster!'**
2. Jack chased Sheng, shouting **'I'm faster!'**

STOP AND THINK
What kind of comma wizardry is at play here?

When I asked a dozen people (young and old), they gave me convincing explanations why they believed it was Jack or Sheng shouting. Although logically it is possible to accept different explanations, there is one grammatical answer after we've checked why a comma appears in the second sentence.

By separating 'Sheng' and 'shouting', the comma gives us a second clause.

 Jack chased Sheng shouting **'I'm faster!'**

 Jack chased Sheng, shouting **'I'm faster!'**

We now have two clauses, in which Jack is the subject. Two different verbs specify what he did or was doing:

1. Jack **chased** Sheng

and:

2. Jack **was shouting** 'I'm faster!'

We could argue whether it is Sheng or Jack who is shouting in sentence 1, but Jack is the shouting boy in sentence 2.

KEY TAKEAWAY

Commas separate clauses to avoid ambiguity (difficulty understanding if there is more than one meaning of the sentence).

Inspecting the verb (checking what question it answers) helps with that.

Commas add clarity.

 **OVER TO YOU**
Can you match the pictures to the correct sentences?

(A)

1. It was a very long zebra crossing.

2. It was a very long zebra, crossing.

It was a very long zebra crossing.

It was a very long zebra, crossing.

(B)

(C)

3. Save him not, kill him.

4. Save him, not kill him.

 Save him not, kill him.

 Save him, not kill him.

(D)

E

5. I'd like building blocks and a puppy for Zeina.

6. I'd like building blocks, and a puppy for Zeina.

 I'd like building blocks and a puppy for Zeina.

 I'd like building blocks, and [I'd like] a puppy for Zeina.

F

THE COMMA HELPS TO AVOID CONCLUSION

I think you mean 'confusion', Zed. Or ambiguity.

11

Main and 'Sub' Clauses

One more try, Zed. You can do it.

AFTER THE TEACHER SAID IT WAS A PIECE OF CAKE

Then?

AFTER THE TEACHER SAID IT WAS A PIECE OF CAKE

Then what, Zed? Is your system crashing again?

TIMMY ATE HIS HOMEWORK

Finally! After only six attempts. Did you like my joke?

WHAT JOKE

The one you just read.

MAKES NO SENSE

You have to think of what the teacher said and what Timmy did.

DOGS EAT HOMEWORK

We'll try another day. If this isn't going to work, perhaps underwater clauses will.

 STOP AND THINK
How many clauses are there in the joke?

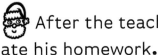 After the teacher said it was a piece of cake, Timmy ate his homework.

Two. Have you noticed that only one can be a sentence in its own right?

 Timmy ate his homework.

The other clause leaves us with questions:

 After the teacher said it was a piece of cake

Then what happened? We need another clause to complete the sentence.

CLAUSE FACTS

Main clause

A clause that can work on its own is called the main clause (or independent clause). It doesn't need another clause to complete or explain it. It can be a sentence in its own right.

Subordinate clause

A clause that can't work on its own is called the subordinate clause (or dependent clause). It can't be a sentence in its own right. It is dependent on another clause to complete or explain it. It completes the main clause. That's why it is somewhat sub-standard.

'Sub' in Latin means 'under', 'below'.

When the **first clause is subordinate**, we **use a comma after it**.

SUBORDINATE IS A LONG WORD

Just today, we can shorten it to 'sub', as in **sub**marine, or **sub**marine sandwich. Yum!

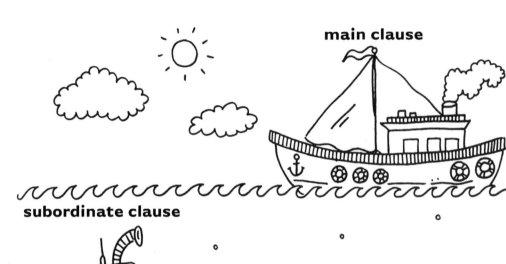

main clause

subordinate clause

Do you remember when I said that clauses, not words, are the building blocks of sentences? I've built a submarine and a ship to show you how the two clauses relate to each other. Look at the arrow pressing the sub down.

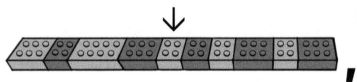

Timmy ate his homework

After the teacher said it was a piece of cake

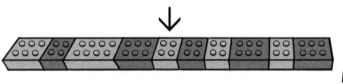

MAIN CLAUSE

SUBORDINATE CLAUSE

When **the first clause is subordinate (sub)**, a comma goes in between the two clauses.

Many sub clauses can be recognised by their first words.

LEMON SQUEEZY

Can you think of sentences that start with the words or word combinations below? They'll have one sub and one main clause. Don't forget to separate the clauses with a comma.

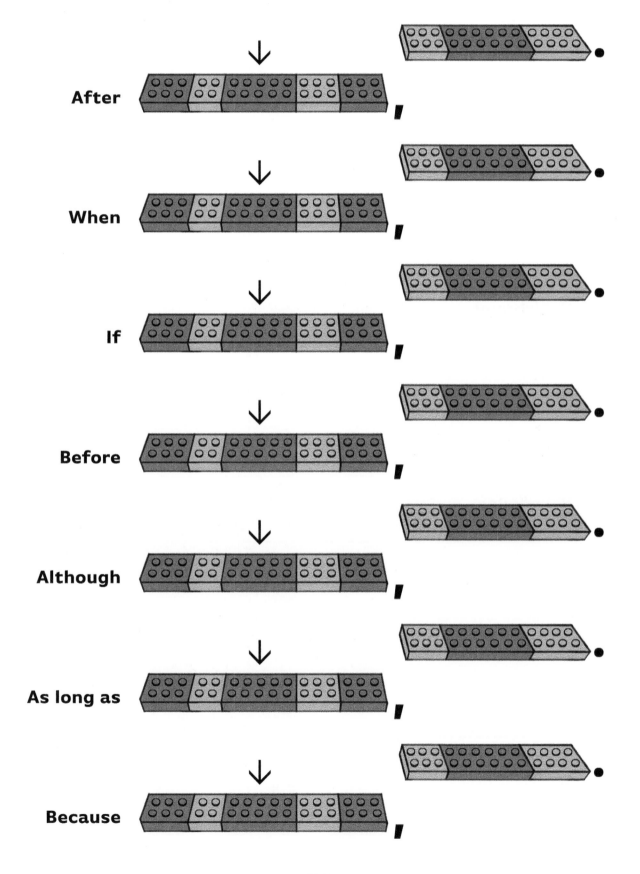

Now write them down:

After I read the comic, I knew I was the superhero.

When _____ , _____
_____ .

If _____ , _____
_____ .

Before _____ , _____
_____ .

Although _____ _____
_____ .

As long as _____ _____
_____ .

Because _____ _____
_____ .

After _____ _____
_____ .

Before _____ _____
_____ .

If _____ _____
_____ .

STEP IT UP
Can you find a **sub clause** in every sentence? Look for **characteristic words** that sub clauses start with. If the sub clause is at the front of the sentence, a comma is needed to separate it from the main clause. If it's at the back, there's no need for a comma in the sentence.

When you spell 'part' backwards**,** it's a trap.

It's a trap **when** you spell 'part' backwards.

After I took a day off**,** I was fired from the calendar factory.

I was fired from the calendar factory **after** I took a day off.

If procrastination was an Olympic sport I'd compete in it later.

When I found out that my toaster wasn't waterproof I was shocked.

You'll thank me after I've done the favour for you.

If every day is a gift I'd like a receipt for Monday – I want to exchange it for another Friday.

As soon as I try to hug someone cuddly my face hits the mirror.

If you're not supposed to eat at night why is there a light bulb in the fridge?

I do unforgettable things when I want to improve my memory.

When the past comes knocking don't answer – it has nothing new to say.

If you run in front of a car you'll get tired. If you run behind the car you'll get exhausted.

When you're right no one remembers. When you're wrong no one forgets.

If we have brains to work out problems why do we use them to create more problems?

Don't look at me when I'm trying to concentrate.

If tomatoes are a fruit is ketchup technically a smoothie?

I stop the microwave one second before the ting because I like to feel like a bomb defuser.

When you repeat the same mistakes for so long you should start calling them traditions.

If you are hotter than me I am cooler than you.

Chocolate is fruit to me because cocoa beans grow on trees.

I like to have a lie in as long as I'm allowed to have one.

If a clean desk is the sign of a clear mind then a clean house is the sign of broken Internet.

When nothing is going right go left.

Don't stop when you're almost there!

If there's the best time to open a gift it is the present.

When there are footprints on the moon don't tell me the sky is the limit.

We conveniently forgot to wash Bertie after we'd taken him for a walk in a muddy park.

If life is not smiling at you give it a good tickling.

Emily asked every guest if they wanted to sponsor her India expedition.

If you can't convince them confuse them.

When your children are young you're a superhero. When they're teens you're a super villain. After that your only power is invisibility.

Although teamwork is overrated it helps to put the blame on someone else.

If time is money cash machines should be called time machines.

When in doubt mumble.

BRING IT ON

Read the sentence below and look at the picture. The writer remembered to put the comma in between the two clauses, but there is a problem with the sentence's meaning. The players do look at the coach. What is the matter?

> When the coach approaches, the players don't look at him.

This question should help: which of the two sentences matches the picture? Check the position of the comma.

> When the coach approaches, the players don't look at him.

> When the coach approaches the players, don't look at him.

Ah... That's clearer.

When the coach approaches, the players don't look at him.

It's not enough to separate the sub and the main clause with a comma. We have to carefully check where the comma is going.

UNLESS YOU WANT YOUR WRITING TO SINK TO THE BOTTOM OF THE SEA

You're quite right there, Zed.

Now that sub clauses make good sense to you, Zed, let me show you another way they can start. Watch out for 'doing' words in the present or past tense, including words ending in -ing and -ed.

Ben wondered if dinner was ready

Peeping through the heavy kitchen door

Peeping through the heavy kitchen door, Ben wondered if dinner was ready.

OVER TO YOU
Can you think of sentences that start with the words or word combinations below? They'll have one sub and one main clause. Don't forget to separate the clauses with a comma.

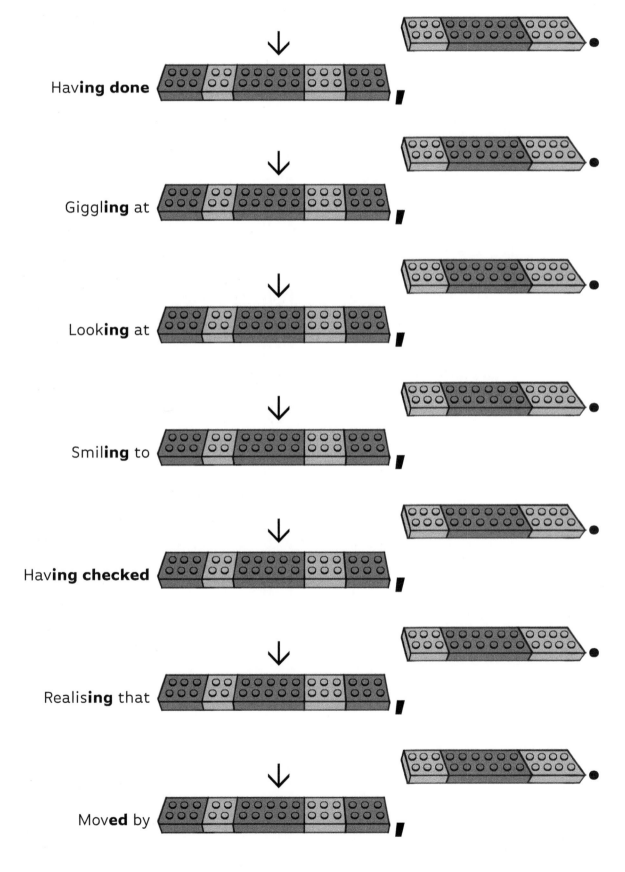

Hav**ing done**

Giggl**ing** at

Look**ing** at

Smil**ing** to

Hav**ing checked**

Realis**ing** that

Mov**ed** by

Now write them down.

Having done two lines of writing, I took an obligatory 5-minute break.

Giggling _____ , _____
_____ .

Looking at_____ , _____
_____ .

Smiling to _____ , _____
_____ .

Having checked _____ _____
_____ .

Realising that _____ _____
_____ .

Moved by _____ _____
_____ .

Having sat_____ _____
_____ .

Struck by_____ _____
_____ .

BREEZE THROUGH
Can you put in missing commas in the sentences below?

Having done her history homework Aisha went running in the park.

Looking through the glass door I wondered if the house was empty.

Helped by Gran I grew impressive tomatoes on the windowsill.

Feeling the pressure the management removed the 'No dogs' sign.

Having heard it was the teacher's birthday Sian wrote a poem for Mrs Brown.

Feeling uneasy I decided not to admit that I never played Minecraft.

Encouraged by all I made the first step into the unknown.

Having run out of paper I used my t-shirt to carry on making notes.

Not knowing what to do we called the reception for help.

Given such an opportunity of course I was going to take it!

Feeling the cold breeze on my face I pondered if winter was on its way.

Having practised the routes for months Marcus was ready for his driving test.

KEY TAKEAWAY

When the first clause is subordinate, we use a comma after it to separate it from the main clause.

Many subordinate clauses can be recognised by their first words or phrases.

Some start with **after, when, if, before, although, as long as, as soon as** and **before**.

Others start with 'doing' words in the present or past tense, including words **ending in -ing and -ed**.

12
Comma after Fronted Adverbials

Of all domestic animals, cats have the most free will. I feed Pebbles at the same time every day, lovingly emptying pouches of succulent cat food into her favourite bowl. But right now, Pebbles is nowhere in sight. I've checked the garden and I've looked in the shed. I even searched the garage. I walked back into the kitchen to find that she had done it again. Quietly, Pebbles ate my lunch.

Quietly, Pebbles ate my lunch.

Cats are like fronted adverbials. They are right there under your nose, at the very front, while you're focusing on a bigger picture. They make you ask questions: where, when and how, which actually makes your life more interesting.

FRONTED MOUSERS ARE LAZY SO THEY HAVE NO DOING WORDS

Correct, Zed. Fronted adverbials don't have a verb; they are not clauses.

I KNEW SANTA WOULDNT HAVE ANYTHING TO DO WITH MOUSERS

FRONTED ADVERBIALS FACTS

These are words and phrases at the beginning of a sentence that describe the action that follows. You can think of the fronted adverbial as an additional information to make the sentence more interesting because they answer questions such as **where**, **when** and **how**.

Fronted adverbials are not clauses because they don't have a verb, or words that act like verbs.

Where?

Upstairs,
Over there,
In the distance,
Here,
Back at the house,
Far away,
Wherever he went,
Nearby,
Under the ground,
Behind the bed,
Outside,
Back at the house,

When?

In February,
Afterwards,
Before long,
All of a sudden,
Today,
Tomorrow,
Immediately,
Just then,
In the evening,
Last week,
On Sunday,
After a little while,

How?

Quietly,
Slowly,
As quick as a flash,
Suddenly,
Without a warning,
As fast as I could,
Barely alive,
Understandably,
Unexpectedly,
Somewhat flustered,
Unbelievably,
Without a word,

COMMA FACTS

Commas are used after fronted adverbials to separate them from the rest of the sentence.

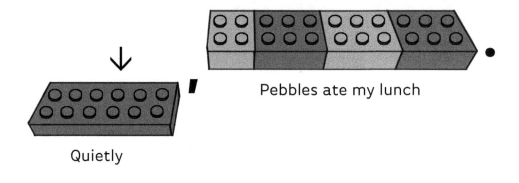

Quietly

Pebbles ate my lunch

STOP AND THINK
Why is it important that fronted adverbials are separated by commas?

We can't assume that the reader knows what we are trying to communicate in our writing. Imagine you've written a passage about ways to travel the world carefree, and someone infers it's about time travellers!

Most of the time, travellers worry about their luggage.

Most of the time travellers worry about their luggage.

ROBOTS WILL TIME TRAVEL BEFORE HUMANS

Humans already do, especially writers. When you add a fronted adverbial to an existing sentence to make it more interesting, it's a bit like going back in time to fix something.

> Mr Baker was on his way.

> As quick as a flash, Mr Baker was on his way.

I wonder why the hurry.

KEY TAKEAWAY

Just like subordinate clauses in the frontal position, fronted adverbials are always separated by a comma.

Without fronted adverbials, sentences are grammatically correct, although might be less interesting to the reader.

OVER TO YOU

Without fronted adverbials, the sentences are not very exciting. Can you turn these into funny, intriguing and even cheeky sentences? Don't forget to use commas.

As quickly as is humanly possible, Dad checked his lottery ticket, then gave out a sigh of disappointment.

Back at the sleepy house, the mice and spiders enjoyed occupying Barry's bedroom in perfect harmony.

. . . . ,   I asked the teacher to speak less loudly when passing my desk.

. . . . ,   Mick Saddler made history by introducing scootering to the school grounds.

. . . .   a procrastinator's work is never done.

. . . .   dogs have more friends because they wag their tails, not their tongues.

. . . .   never trust a dog to watch your food.

. . . .   a true friend gives his paw, not his hand.

. . . .   rabbits make good house pets.

. . . .   the trolley went sideways and hit the shelves.

. . . .   the neighbours ran through the field.

. . . .   the milkman made a strange delivery.

. . . .   we declined the invitation.

. . . .   Pebbles jumped onto Mum's bed.

. . . .   I wasn't even there!

LEMON SQUEEZY
Now it's your chance to be creative with sentences' endings. Don't forget to put in missing commas.

On the other hand, you have different fingers.

To his amazement, ...

First of all . . . .

Secondly . . . .

Politely . . . .

Anyway . . . .

Earlier . . . .

On the whole . . . .

With a wave . . . .

Unfortunately . . . .

As fast as they could . . . .

Quietly . . . .

In due course . . . .

More than ever . . . .

As a result . . . .

In contrast . . . .

In complete disbelief . . . .

To be absolutely honest . . . .

13

Commas 'Hugging' a Subordinate Clause

Tom is Mr Kowalski's best student. There isn't a quadratic expression that he can't factorise in his head. Once all classwork is done and dusted – usually within minutes – Tom looks for fresh sources of entertainment. He has just left the classroom to change locker codes in accordance with today's algebraic equations. It took Mr Kowalski two hours to help students open their lockers. Tom's bold prank, although intended to be harmless, cost him detention.

Tom's bold prank, although intended to be harmless, cost him detention.

 STOP AND THINK
How many clauses are there in the sentence?

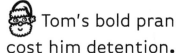 Tom's bold prank, although intended to be harmless, cost him detention.

Main clause: Tom's bold prank cost him detention
Subordinate clause: although intended to be harmless

121

Tom's bold prank ▌ cost him detention ●

although intended to be harmless ▌

Look at that poor subordinate clause, pushed down. We've given it two commas to hug it, so it feels better.

HUGGING IS OVERRATED
YOU CAN GET AN ELECTRIC SHOCK

The subordinate clause is extra information. We know this because the sentence would still work if we removed it. Without cutting it off, we use commas to separate it from the rest of the sentence.

KEY TAKEAWAY

When the subordinate clause (with additional information) is inserted inside the sentence, use a comma before and after the clause.

When the separated part (by commas) is taken out, the sentence should still work, as if the extra information was never there.

Think **additional information**, think **separated by commas**.

BREEZE THROUGH

Can you find all subordinate clauses and give them 'hugging' commas in these sentences?

In two weeks if he takes the medicine regularly he'll be good as new.

Sam and Kay feeling exhausted from fixing the computer bug decided to call it a day.

Abi's biggest secret if we agree that toddlers can keep secrets was finally out.

Suri's decision because she believed in kindness over adventure was that the dog was reunited with its owner.

Tom's revelation after he's finally let the cat out of the bag is that he hates furry animals.

It was Rhona and Geeta who having completed the first aid course announced their decision to become army medics.

In hindsight although my friends begged me I shouldn't have gone to the party.

My devotion for my dog after I bought a toddler pushchair for him was completely slated by other people.

Martha feeling guilty for what she had done stood up to make an announcement.

No prizes for guessing though this is quite a clever Sherlock episode who the killer is.

The school's parent committee as long as it's in operation in August is welcome to attend the event.

Miss Jones' holiday while we appreciate your concerns has already been accepted.

Elizabeth while still grieving her father's death was crowned the new monarch.

14

Relative Clauses and Puppies

Jon follows Instagram pages with pictures of cute puppies. Scientists in Japan would be pleased with Jon. They encourage people to enjoy images of baby animals because exposure to *kawaii* (cute, adorable and lovable things) sharpens our focus. Just imagine how well Jon should do in class tests and exams after looking at all the pictures of cute puppies! Sadly, Jon is yet to appreciate the value of regular revision.

Jon has a test on relative clauses in English next week. What better way to help him with revision than combining it with pictures of cute puppies?

I have five adorable puppies in my garden. Have you noticed anything different about the one in the sandpit?

The puppy that is in the sandpit is quite fluffy.

The puppy is fluffier than the other puppies. And it's the only one actually sitting in the sandpit.

Of all the puppies, which one is quite fluffy?

The one that is in the sandpit.

Here, the middle clause ('that is in the sandpit') defines the subject (puppy). It's an important piece of information.

Now, let's pretend there's only one puppy in my garden.

The puppy**, which is in the sandpit,** is quite fluffy**.**

What is special about the puppy?

It's quite fluffy.

Here, the middle clause ('which is in the sandpit') doesn't define the subject (puppy). It is extra information – as there is only one quite fluffy puppy, we don't need to provide its specific location. If the puppy were under my rose bush, it wouldn't have made a real difference, as I'm focusing on the fact that it is fluffy.

RELATIVE CLAUSE FACTS

Relative clause is a type of subordinate clause.

Defining relative clause specifies what the sentence is talking about. It is connected to the main clause by the word **that**.
Don't use commas to separate this clause.

Non-defining relative clause adds additional information to the sentence. If removed, the sentence still makes sense. It is connected to the main clause by the words **which, who, whom** or **whose**. If the clause were cut off, the sentence would still work.
Use commas to separate this clause.

The defining and non-defining relative clauses make more sense when we label our puppy pictures.

defining relative clause

The puppy that is in the sandpit is quite fluffy.

non-defining
relative
clause

The puppy**, which is in the sandpit,** is quite fluffy.

We can use building blocks to see how non-defining relative clauses work.

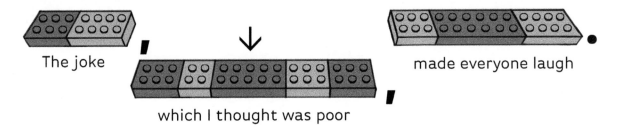

See how the two commas 'hug' the sub clause.

The joke, which I thought was poor, made everyone laugh.

 OVER TO YOU
How can we change the non-defining relative clause in the above sentence to a defining one?

The joke that I thought was poor made everyone laugh.

STOP AND THINK
Does the new sentence have a different meaning?

No better way to compare the two sentences than by putting them side by side in a table.

The joke, **which I thought was poor**, made everyone laugh.	The joke **that I thought was poor** made everyone laugh.
There was only one joke told.	There was more than one joke told.
The fact that the joke was poor is extra information.	The fact that the joke was poor is important – it distinguishes this joke from the other jokes.
Non-specific information = **non-defining clause**	*Specific information =* **defining clause**
We **can't** use 'that' instead of 'which' (or 'who' in other examples).	We **can** use 'that' and 'which', although 'that' is more commonly used.

THE HUMAN WHO BROKE THE ROBOT KEPT PUSHING ALL THE BUTTONS

That is correct, Zed. No commas needed, although a full stop should complete the sentence. Was that any human we know?

TWO OUT OF THREE HUMANS IN EVERY ELECTRONICS SHOP

KEY TAKEAWAY

When sub clauses start with the words 'that', 'which', 'who', 'whom' or 'whose', they are called **relative clauses**.

Defining relative clauses are connected to the main clause by the word 'that' (no commas to separate them).

Non-defining relative clauses are connected to the main clause by the words 'which', 'who', 'whom' or 'whose' (commas separate them). These clauses add additional information to the sentence.

STEP IT UP

Correct or incorrect sentence? Check the pronouns (**that, who, whom, which**) before deciding if commas are needed.

✓ _____ People who walk in circles are wondering what they've forgotten.

✗ _____ The bus stop, that we just passed, is always very busy.

_____ The recipe which we haven't tried before seems easy to follow.

_____ Ali, who scored four goals, is the new captain of the team.

_____ The jokes that I dislike the most start with 'Knock, knock...'

_____ Mr Blake, which is our neighbour, is a keen gardener.

_____ We left Biscuit, that was asleep in his cage, with Mrs Shelley.

_____ Children, who don't stop smiling, will be let into the tent first.

_____ The fruit, which we got from Ella, made the cake sweet and rich.

_____ Cold-blooded animals that have scaly skin are called reptiles.

_____ The painting that I forgot to mention in my essay is by Monet.

_____ The answer, that was actually incorrect, earned the team a point.

TAKE A BOW
Only one of the three sentence options matches the description in bold. Which one?

Not all customers are shocked. Only the ones who find out I'm a bad electrician.

✓_____ Customers who find out I'm a bad electrician are shocked.

✗_____ Customers, who find out I'm a bad electrician, are shocked.

✗_____ Customers, that find out I'm a bad electrician, are shocked.

I have many books. The one I'm interested in is about anti-gravity.

_____ The book, that is about anti-gravity, is impossible to put down.

_____ The book, which is about anti-gravity, is impossible to put down.

_____ The book that is about anti-gravity is impossible to put down.

Adam did only one prank and the prank involved swapping tickets.

_____ Adam's prank that involved swapping tickets can't be undone.

_____ Adam's prank, which involved swapping tickets, can't be undone.

_____ Adam's prank, that involved swapping tickets, can't be undone.

Although I have many dogs, only my German Shepherd guards me at night.

_____ The dog, which guards me at night, is my German Shepherd.

_____ The dog that guards me at night is my German Shepherd.

_____ The dog, who guards me at night, is my German Shepherd.

Only one diagnosis was made. It came out of the blue.

_____ The diagnosis, which came out of the blue, was colour blindness.

_____ The diagnosis, that came out of the blue, was colour blindness.

_____ The diagnosis that came out of the blue was colour blindness.

15

Two or More Main Clauses

This year's comedy festival at Dowell Academy was a memorable one. Roy's joke 'The headteacher told me to have a good day, so I went home' made Mr Singh chuckle so vigorously that he spilt water on the other judges' laps. Sid was disqualified because his unoriginal entry 'I once gave Elsa a balloon, but she let it go' was, in Mr Singh's words, 'all over the Internet'. It was Priscilla's pun that the jury unanimously declared the most hard-hitting: 'I know I'm a handful, but that's why teachers have two hands.'

 STOP AND THINK
How many clauses are there in each one-liner?

 The headteacher told me to have a good day, so I went home.

 I once gave Elsa a balloon, but she let it go.

 I know I'm a handful, but that's why teachers have two hands.

 STOP AND THINK
Can you find a subordinate clause in each sentence? Why?

There is no subordinate clause in any of the sentences. Each clause can be a sentence in its own right.

I CAN SEE SHIPS BUT NOT A SINGLE SUBMARINE

CLAUSE FACTS

A clause that can work on its own in the sentence is called **the main clause** (or independent clause). It can be a sentence in its own right.

I once gave Elsa a balloon

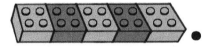

but she let it go

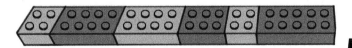

MAIN CLAUSE

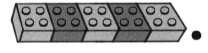

MAIN CLAUSE

COMMA FACTS

When there are two (or more) main clauses connected by **conjunctions** (words such as 'and', 'or', 'but', 'so' and 'yet'), we often use a comma to separate them.

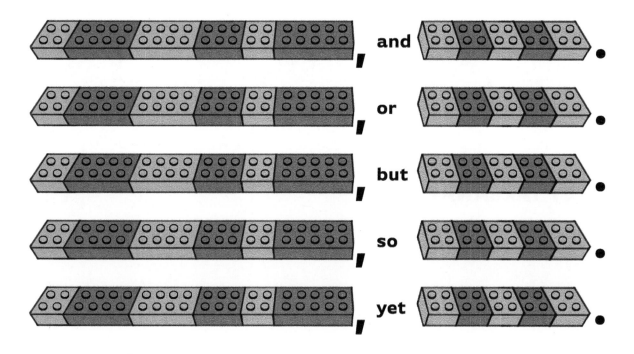

Now look at a sentence with more than two main clauses. The rule for using the comma(s) is the same.

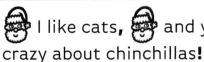 I like cats, and you clearly love dogs, but Mia is crazy about chinchillas!

I like cats

and you clearly love dogs

but Mia is crazy about chinchillas

MAIN CLAUSE

MAIN CLAUSE

MAIN CLAUSE

KEY TAKEAWAY

When there are two or more main clauses in a sentence, we often separate them by commas.

You will recognise such sentences, as the clauses will be connected by words such as 'and', 'or', 'but', 'so' and 'yet'.

The commas add clarity to the sentence.

 OVER TO YOU

Can you separate the main clauses using commas? Start by looking for connecting words (conjunctions).

Don't ask me anything and I won't tell you any lies.

Money doesn't grow on trees yet banks have branches.

Dad and I laugh about how competitive we are but I laugh more.

I may not have lost all my marbles yet but there is a small hole in the bag somewhere.

I started out with nothing and I still have most of it.

A computer once beat me at chess but it was no match for me at kick boxing.

My pencil supposedly belonged to Shakespeare but I can't tell if it's 2B or not 2B.

We can't help everyone but everyone can help someone.

We can watch 'Batman' or we can watch 'Batman Returns'.

I used to think that I was indecisive but now I'm not too sure.

Never let a fool kiss you or a kiss fool you.

Cats spend two thirds of their lives sleeping and the other third making viral videos.

A garage sale is actually a garbage sale but the 'b' is silent.

Andy's resolution was to read more so he put the subtitles on TV.

Grandad says he always wanted to be somebody but he now realised he should have been more specific.

We like birthdays yet we forget that too many will kill us.

I'd tell you a chemistry joke but I know I wouldn't get a reaction.

The puzzle said 3–5 years yet I finished it in 18 months.

You can lead a horse to water but you can't make it drink.

I wouldn't normally press F5 but it's so refreshing.

The early bird catches the worm but the second mouse gets the cheese.

It may look like I'm doing nothing yet in my head I'm very busy.

I'm not saying I'm a superhero but have you seen me and Batman together in the same place at the same time?

My opinions may have changed but not the fact that I am right.

Change is inevitable but not from a vending machine.

16

Commas – Putting It All Together

What have we learned about the not-so-humble comma?

Of all the punctuation marks, the comma is:

1. the second most frequently used (after the full stop)

2. one of the most confusing and least known about (alongside the semicolon)

3. entrusted with a whole range of different **grammatical functions**:
   - listing people and things
   - separating names
   - separating clauses in ambiguous sentences
   - separating subordinate clauses in frontal positions
   - 'hugging' subordinate clauses in middle positions
   - separating fronted adverbials
   - separating non-defining relative clauses
   - separating two or more main clauses.

PLAIN ENGLISH PLEASE

The comma separates and organises information, so the reader gets the right sentence meaning.

APPROACHING SYSTEM OVERLOAD ERROR

I have just the right visual aid for you – The Comma Blueprint.

 STOP AND THINK
What grammatical function does each part of the Comma Blueprint illustrate? The list of bullet points on the previous page will help.

The Comma Blueprint

Xxxx, xxxx, xxxx, xxxx **and** xxxx.

Xxxx xxxx xxxx xxxx, **Name.**

Name, xxxx xxxx xxxx xxxx xxxx**?**

X xxxx xxxx xxxx xxxx zebra crossing.

X xxxx xxxx xxxx xxxx zebra, crossing.

↓

When xxxx xxxx, xxxx xxxx xxxx xxxx xxx.

If xxxx xxxx, xxxx xxxx xxxx xxxx xxx.

Seeing xxxx xxxx, xxxx xxxx xxxx xxxx xxx.

Having seen xxxx xxxx, xxxx xxxx xxxx xxxx xxx.

↓

Xxxx xxxx xxxx, xxxx xxxx xxxx xxxx, xxxx xxxx xxxx.

Quietly, xxxx xxxx xxxx.

Before long, xxxx xxxx xxxx.

As fast as I could, xxxx xxxx xxxx.

↓

Xxxx xxxx xxxx, **which** xxxx xxxx xxxx, xxxx xxxx xxxx.

Xxxx xxxx xxxx, **who** xxxx xxxx xxxx, xxxx xxxx xxxx.

Xxxx xxxx xxxx, **whom** xxxx xxxx xxxx, xxxx xxxx xxxx.

Xxxx xxxx xxxx, **or** xxxx xxxx xxxx.

Xxxx xxxx xxxx, **and** xxxx xxxx xxxx, **but** xxxx xxxx xxxx.

Xxxx xxxx xxxx, **yet** xxxx xxxx xxxx, **so** xxxx xxxx xxxx.

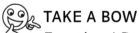 **TAKE A BOW**

Fun time! Referring to The Comma Blueprint, use building blocks, sticks, pasta pieces, pens/pencils, rulers and any other everyday objects to make visual representations of the structure of different sentences. Why not use raisins for commas and peas for full stops? You can draw the remaining punctuation marks.

Reminder: The main clause can be a sentence in its own right, but the subordinate clause (sub) can't – it completes the main clause.

Although they are birds penguins cannot fly.

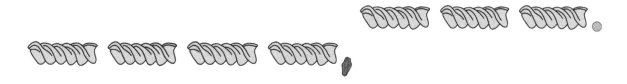

I wouldn't call that unusual Mr Holmes.

The maths test which is actually tomorrow is too easy to revise for.

After my teacher called me average I told him it was mean!

People say nothing is impossible but I do nothing every day.

Lisa has your missing cat been found yet?

None of my books which are all arranged alphabetically by the author is by Dom Harris.

Having burned 3,000 calories I vowed to never leave cake in the oven while napping.

My opinions may have changed but not the fact that I'm right.

Rightfully the man who invented the windowsill is a ledge.

Without ME even if everyone else was at the party it was just AWESO.

When Dad was a child family dinners came with two options: take it or leave it.

Run as fast as you can Loki and tell everyone Grandad is here.

To be honest I wanted a fridge magnet not six new fridges!

Marley sat at the front so I sat next to him but Al pretended not to see us.

Ollie opened the door cautiously looked inside took his shoes off and tiptoed upstairs.

If you get a letter full of rice it's from Uncle Ben.

The dog chased the cyclist making weird noises. (*The dog, not the cyclist, was making weird noises.*)

The postman who lives next door knows our dog really well.

I decided to have Moses Leah Seth Noah Harry and Aria on my team.

Before long the secret art project was completed but Miss Chen had another surprise for us.

I wouldn't say I'm good at athletics having come last in my class but I enjoy taking part.

I'd like some Banoffee pie and ice cream for Freya. (*I'd like some Banoffee pie for me, and ice cream for Freya.*)

That would never happen would it?

You ask my opinion yet you're upset when I give it to you.

Greta Thunberg whom we never met in person inspired us the most.

Because the wind is very strong we're wearing extra layers and raincoats.

After meeting Jaxon Sian realised what was missing in her life so she set up a new charity.

Did the shop have carrots onions leeks or parsnips?

Because they're always up to something staircases should never be trusted.

Evening news although starting with 'Good evening' always leaves people with a worse evening than before they sat down to watch it.

That was my final answer but the teacher kept asking me more questions.

Listening to a song about a tortilla Mo knew it was a rap.

Elsie did you remember to get flour eggs and milk on the way from school?

If I promise to miss you will you go now?

The graffiti student whose name cannot be revealed called himself the Young Banksy of Merseyside.

Driving too fast Dad struggled to find the way out.

Shall I do it now wait until tomorrow or not do it at all?

17

Colon

 STOP AND THINK
Are these emojis or emoticons?

Emojis are small images inserted into text – you'll be familiar with tens of yellow faces on your smartphone. However, emojis are not simply facial expressions; they can be pictures of flags, food, animals, activities and occupations, to name a few.

Emoticons are much simpler facial expressions made with keyboard characters. They made plain text messages more entertaining well before smartphones started listing emojis.

:/

What are you not sure about, Zed?

IF YOU KNOW WHAT :/ MEAN

Hang on a minute. Zed, you've just used punctuation marks for the first time!

YOU SAID THEY WERE EMOTICONS

You know what that means? All I have to do to teach you punctuation is to use keyboard combinations that look like face pictures.

((_ _)) ..zzzZZZ.. ..zzzZZZ..

Is that a maybe?

It seems that Zed would have no problem telling the meanings of the emoticons at the top of this section. Can you? They all have one punctuation mark in common: the colon. Zed called it 'the eyes' once, which makes sense when you think what the colon's job actually is.

The colon is used **BEFORE WRITING A LIST.**

 LOOK!

 THESE ARE THE PEOPLE OR ITEMS I'M LISTING...

The headteacher asked for three children : Ella, Harry and Fatima.

Only four colours are stocked : blue, green, grey and brown.

Who was quicker : Bella or Freddie?

The colon is also used to **GIVE EXAMPLES OR MORE EXPLANATION** in a sentence.

◐ LOOK!

◐ HERE'S MORE INFORMATION TO MAKE IT CLEARER...

'Harry Potter' is my favourite book **:** it has magic, friendship and courage all in one place.

This programme is short and animated **:** it is for young children.

When giving examples or more explanation, we sometimes turn a sentence into a joke.

◐ **)** LOOK!

◐ THIS LOOKS LIKE A GOOD ONE-LINER...

The shortest horror story **:** Monday.

Never let anyone treat you like regular glue **:** you're glitter glue.

I'm on a seafood diet: I see food, and I eat it.

Campers: Mother Nature's way of feeding mosquitos.

Finally, a colon can be used to START A QUOTATION in a sentence.

 LOOK!

 A QUOTATION FOLLOWS...

Mark Twain said : 'Never regret anything that made you smile.'

COLON FACTS

There is no white space before the word and the colon.

The colon is followed by a single white space, never a hyphen.

If you've seen these combinations, they are incorrect.

:-   **-:**

Don't use them in your own writing.

 OVER TO YOU
Can you put in all missing punctuation marks?

Secret something that is told to one person at a time

Mum's announcement today 'Happy 10-week anniversary to the 28 browser tabs I have open'

Anger the feeling that makes your mouth work faster than your mind

I was picked for my motivational skills everyone always says they have to work twice as hard when I'm around

My teenagers are optimists every glass they leave around the house is at least half full

Insanity doing the same thing over and over again and expecting different results

Be a pineapple stand tall wear a crown and be sweet on the inside

To the guy who invented the zero thanks for nothing

Determination taking a lot of steps to avoid lifts

Some people are like Slinkies they don't do much all day but you can't help smiling when you see one tumble down the stairs

The shinbone a device for finding furniture in a dark room

Keep the dream alive hit the snooze button

To people who write 'u' instead of 'you' what do you do with all the time you save?

Dad's life complaint laugh and the world laughs with you but snore and you sleep alone

KEY TAKEAWAY

The colon introduces information in a sentence.

Use it before a list, an example or explanation, or a quotation.

18

Semicolon

The semicolon is the colon's 'winking' relative.

It's also a well-known prankster. It gets students into trouble when they can't remember what it actually does! Luckily, like milk, all pranks have their 'best by' date. Do you know what happened to the semicolon?

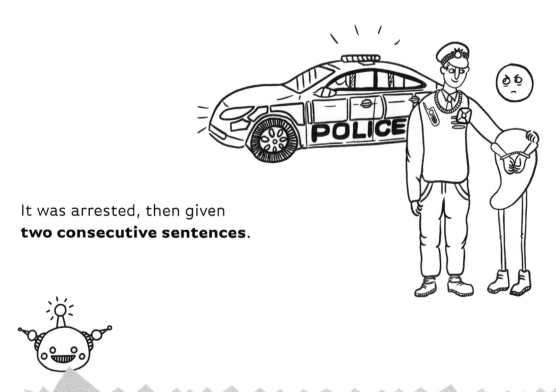

It was arrested, then given **two consecutive sentences**.

CONSECUTIVE MEANS ONE AFTER ANOTHER

Correct. Since the semicolon's job is to join two sentences together (merge them as one), this couldn't be a more fitting penalty. But only when both sentences are strongly connected in meaning and are of equal importance (are main clauses).

Russian dolls are not very popular.
They are too full of themselves.

Russian dolls are not very popular; they are too full of themselves.

 STOP AND THINK
How do we know that two sentences are strongly connected in meaning?

The second sentence usually explains the first one. By connecting them with a semicolon, we draw the reader's attention to the link between them.

In some cases, the semicolon works as well as the full stop. It is the writer who decides which punctuation mark is more appropriate.

If the writer creates suspense, then the full stop works well. If they aim to provide explanation to the first main clause, the semicolon is better suited.

Don't press your luck; you might pop it.

Don't press your luck; you might pop it.

The semicolon can be exchangeable with the full stop but it is never completely optional. Just look at Bryan, full of guilt and sorrow.

Without the semicolon, we are changing the mood dramatically... What happened to Bryan's guilt and sorrow now?

 **OVER TO YOU**

Lottie is confused. She's been given advice about which pet to save money for, but the message came in capital letters and without punctuation: HAVE A HAMSTER IF YOU CANT HAVE A CAT.

WHY LOOK AT ME

No reason, Zed.

Did the sender suggest a hamster or a cat?

There are two possibilities:

1. a cat is preferred, but if it's not possible, then a hamster is a good second choice

2. a hamster is preferred, but if it's not possible, then a cat is a good second choice.

STEP IT UP

Can you match the images to their correctly punctuated messages?

(A)

1. Have a hamster if you can't have a cat.

2. Have a hamster; if you can't, have a cat.

(B)

A semicolon is also used in lists with longer phrases. Compare these two lists:

> Please buy milk, bread, flour and jam.

> The shopping list included: two pints of semi-skimmed milk; one loaf of brown bread; a bag of plain flour; and a jar of premium quality strawberry jam.

Semicolons in longer lists with more 'wordy' items help separate the items more efficiently so the reader is not confused.

 LEMON SQUEEZY
Can you put in missing punctuation marks in these two lists?

Please buy a suitcase Levi jacket vase and a bus ticket

Please buy a suitcase big enough to pack all your belongings a Levi jacket to replace the one you have helped yourself to in my wardrobe a vase that looks exactly like the one you broke yesterday and a bus ticket that will take you back to Aunt Jo

WHAT'S THE LONGEST SENTENCE WITH SEMICOLONS?

While there might be many contenders, one has to admire Charles Dickens for fitting as many as six semicolons in one long sentence at the beginning of 'Great Expectations':

> At such a time I found out for certain that this bleak place overgrown with nettles was the churchyard; and that Philip Pirrip, late of this parish, and also Georgiana wife of the above, were dead and buried; and that Alexander, Bartholomew, Abraham, Tobias, and Roger, infant children of the aforesaid, were also dead and buried; and that the dark flat wilderness beyond the churchyard, intersected with dikes and mounds and gates, with scattered cattle feeding on it, was the marshes; and that the low leaden line beyond was the river; and that the distant savage lair from which the wind was rushing was the sea; and that the small bundle of shivers growing afraid of it all and beginning to cry, was Pip.

Six main clauses, each as important as the next one, all packed into one sentence. But don't be tempted to repeat such an achievement, or your writing may be difficult to understand. The particular literary style is best appreciated from a reading, not writing, position.

KEY TAKEAWAY

The semicolon separates two sentences that are strongly connected in meaning and equal in importance (both are main clauses).

It's also used in lists to separate longer (more wordy) phrases.

There is no white space before the word and the semicolon.

The semicolon is followed by a single white space.

BREEZE THROUGH
Can you put in all missing punctuation marks?

I explained the word 'many' to my sister it means a lot to her

Some people feel the rain others just get wet

Knowledge is knowing a tomato is a fruit wisdom is not putting it in a fruit salad

I hate insect puns they really bug me

Intelligence is like underwear you need it but you don't have to show it off.

It was the best of times it was the worst of times

Entries are wide exits are narrow

Our PE teacher has a ticket to the match he hasn't missed a single game for ten years

Sometimes I tuck my knees into my chest and lean forward that's just how I roll

When I was young there were only 25 letters in the alphabet nobody knew why

I hated my job as an origami teacher there was too much paperwork

I'm working on a device that will read minds I'd love to hear your thoughts

I have two hemispheres in the left one there's nothing right in the right one there's nothing left

There are three kinds of people the ones who learn by reading the ones who learn by observation and the rest of them who have to touch the fire to learn it's hot

19

Dash

What did one laced shoe say to the other laced shoe?

Velcro – what a rip-off**!**

DASH FACTS

The dash introduces additional information in **informal sentences**. It does what a comma and semicolon do in more formal writing.

For example:

Informal
Outdoor play is good for you – especially if you're into biking.
Formal
Outdoor play is good for you, especially if you are into biking.

Informal
We've found the keys – we can leave the house!
Formal
We have found the keys; we can leave the house!

Kieran wants to be a nurse. He has learned to spell tricky medical terms, including 'mucus', 'defaecation', 'anaemia', 'haemorrhage' and 'diarrhoea' – in case he has to take fast notes. Kieran uses memory triggers (mnemonics) to recall the spellings. For 'diarrhoea', he writes down the first letter of each word in the sentence: '**D**ash **i**n **a** **r**eal **r**ush – **h**urry, **o**r **e**lse **a**ccident.'

Dash in a real rush **–** hurry**,** or else accident**!**

IF I HAD A STOMACH IT WOULD BE TURNING RIGHT NOW

From laughing, I hope? You may not like it, but your memory does. Mnemonics have to be memorable to work, Zed!

Kieran uses the same technique to tell a dash from a hyphen. The two punctuation marks are both horizontal lines, although not equal in length. He whispers under his breath, 'There's a real rush in a dash' to remind himself that the dash leaves a longer trail on paper.

dash

hyphen

Don't forget there's a space on either side of the dash, which isn't the case for the shorter punctuation mark.

Xxxx xxxx xxxx — xxxx xxxx xxxx.

space   space

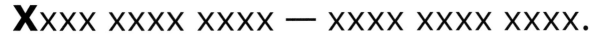

ALL CLEAR GOTTA DASH NOW

Make sure you dash in a real rush!

KEY TAKEAWAY

The dash is used in less formal writing in exactly the same way that commas and semicolons are used. It shows where clauses begin or end. It links strongly linked sentences.

The dash is not to be confused with a hyphen.

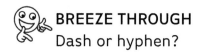

BREEZE THROUGH
Dash or hyphen?

Not everyone likes maths – no point arguing about that! . . . . . dash . . . .

It was a short-lived hope. . . . . hyphen . . . .

I've found the tickets – it was the best day ever! . . . .

The place wasn't just good – it was perfect. . . . .

She's such a happy-go-lucky girl. . . . .

Mum works part-time. . . . .

What happened was incredible – or so we thought. . . . .

At a close-up, it wasn't as scary as we thought it was. . . . .

I'm just trying to be open-minded about the new bistro. . . . .

I think – actually, I believe – we should stand up to him. . . . .

Why won't people admit their faults**?** I would **–** if I had any.

 LEMON SQUEEZY
Can you re-write the sentences so they all have correct punctuation marks?

I can always tell when my brother is lying his lips move

. . . .

. . . .

My cousin has just found out I swapped his bed for a trampoline he hit the roof

. . . .

. . . .

My mother has terrible memory she never forgets anything

. . . .

. . . .

I decided to take up jogging especially as it's Lola's favourite sport

. . . .

. . . .

I prefer chocolate to fruity desserts you can't go wrong with brownies

. . . .

. . . .

All students did well in the rehearsal the teachers were very excited

. . . .

. . . .

Keep smiling it makes people wonder what you have been up to

. . . .

. . . .

I heard a voice inside me say 'Smile! Things could be worse' so I smiled and they did get worse

. . . .

. . . .

This is the best rollercoaster you'll ever sit in hands down

. . . .

. . . .

Everyone everywhere is within walking distance it only depends on how much time you have

. . . .

. . . .

War doesn't tell us who is right only who is left

. . . .

. . . .

Grandad said he had never grown up he had only learned how to act in public

. . . .

. . . .

20
Brackets

After the sudden rainfall, I wasn't sure if the big match was still on. Eve said she would ask her PE teacher (the tall one) whether it was postponed, or was going ahead as planned. She got back to say the match was on. Happy days!

Eve asked her PE teacher **(the tall one)** about the match.

 STOP AND THINK
Why is 'the tall one' in brackets?

HE IS AN IMPORTANT PERSON

Definitely not the reason, Zed.

BUT HE IS CLOSEST TO THE RAIN CLOUDS

It's actually the opposite of being closest to something or being important. **Anything we put in brackets is additional information – it's there, but it might well be left out.** The sentence reads perfectly well and means the same without the text in brackets:

> Eve asked her PE teacher about the match.

SO I READ THE EXTRA WORDS FOR NOTHING

Eve wanted to give all the details: the crucial ones and the less important ones, so I had a full picture in my mind.

Imagine I went into school to speak to the PE department about my attendance at the match. Because Eve gave me the extra information, I would know exactly who to speak to.

AND ASK FOR A WEATHER FORECAST FOR NEXT WEEK

I'm alarmed by your inappropriate sense of humour, Zed. Remind me... Yes, I know, you're not Alexa.

STOP AND THINK
You may want to use brackets at the end of a sentence. Where will you put the final punctuation mark: inside or outside the brackets?

> Whatever you do, always give one hundred per cent (unless you're donating blood**).**

> Whatever you do, always give one hundred per cent (unless you're donating blood**.)**

Do the brackets contain a full sentence? Let's see: 'unless you're donating blood' is a clause, not a full sentence. **The comma goes outside the brackets because the full stop punctuates the whole sentence.**

> Whatever you do, always give one hundred per cent (unless you're donating blood**).**

> Whatever you do, always give one hundred per cent (unless you're donating blood**.)**

 NOW TRY THIS
Can you re-write the sentence so the brackets contain a full sentence and the full stop goes inside the brackets?

> Whatever you do, always give one hundred per cent. **(**This does not apply if you're donating blood**.)**

Perfect.

THIS DOES NOT APPLY IF YOUR PUNCTUATION SOFTWARE UPDATE
IS DELAYED

Oh, Zed. Don't be afraid of learning slowly; be afraid of standing still. (A Chinese proverb, I think.)

GIVE A ROBOT THE RIGHT SOFTWARE AND IT WILL GIVE ONE HUNDRED
PER CENT

I'll call the engineers again this afternoon. (They haven't replied to any of my messages yet.)

BRACKETS AND PUNCTUATION FACTS

If the brackets contain **a full sentence**, the final punctuation mark goes **inside the brackets**.

If the brackets contain a word, phrase or a clause, but **not a full sentence**, the final punctuation mark goes **outside the brackets**, so that it punctuates the whole sentence.

KEY TAKEAWAY

Brackets are used to add additional information in a sentence, for example greater detail or explanation.

The added information is not essential. When removed, the meaning of the sentence is unchanged.

 OVER TO YOU

Can you put in all missing pairs of brackets?

The best way to destroy an enemy apart from a battlefield one is to make them a friend.

Dad cooked lasagne my favourite dinner with four pasta layers.

It's fine if you disagree with me I can't force you to be right.

I thought you'd be interested to know forgive me if you're not that Aidan has a new girlfriend.

Nobody came to Emma's party, which you've guessed it started even earlier than the previous one.

Intelligent people are full of doubt I think.

If I agreed with you hypothetically, we'd both be wrong.

Joseph the boy who has a crush on me delivers newspapers to our house!

I stood up and hiccupped that's not weird, is it?

My French teacher the one with a motor in her mouth confused me like I've never been confused before.

Jo's pasta bake what I prefer to call 'mystery food' went down like a lead balloon.

Reading all sorts of books apart from Facebook gives you wisdom in later life.

I loved every moment and I'm not easily entertained!

STEP IT UP

Decide which punctuation marks (brackets or commas) would improve these sentences or, in some cases, make them correct.

Don't just walk in and take my time unless there's chocolate in your bag.

The cleverest of all in my teacher's opinion is the student who calls themselves a fool at least once a month.

You are pretty close to perfect when you're standing next to me.

Sometimes the cleverest thing and you'll know this from experience is to say nothing at all.

Do you remember John my sister's boyfriend?

Myles came to the party. Do you remember him from school? He was the real life and soul of the party!

I took a calculated risk though I'm bad at maths and it backfired spectacularly.

I wore my army surplus jacket. My date thought I looked tidy!

In moments like this one when the whole flock is out of order the farmer sends a distress message to his sheepdog.

I'll definitely help you with the essay even though there's no moral ground for it.

Barack Obama the former US president will be visiting the museum in May.

I've adopted three stick insects. My brother doesn't know yet!

My family misbehaved at the party as always!

21

Parenthesis

Every time Jake wanted to tell Ella that he liked her, the words would get stuck in his throat. He tried not to stare at Ella in class, which was hard when the teacher's words somehow took the shape and sound of Ella's name. It was the class party last Friday and I was there. I saw Jake (looking dapper) ask Ella to dance. And do you know what?

ALL YOU NEED IS LOVE

Erm... More like, good music. They both rocked on the dance floor!

LOOKING DAPPER IS IN BRACKETS

You'll remember that's because it's additional information that could have been left out. I included it to make Jake a more exciting character.

> I saw Jake **(**looking dapper**)** ask Ella to dance**.**

What I want to show you is that, whether I had used brackets, commas, or dashes, I would have achieved pretty much the same effect:

> I saw Jake **(**looking dapper**)** ask Ella to dance**.**
>
> I saw Jake**,** looking dapper**,** ask Ella to dance**.**
>
> I saw Jake **–** looking dapper **–** ask Ella to dance**.**

The phrase 'looking dapper' is **parenthesis** – words inserted into a sentence to add information. Its purpose is to explain something, or to elaborate on something, providing more details.

If we leave the parenthesis out, the sentence should 'work' without it.

In your own writing, remember that **dashes are best used in informal expressions**. When writing in school books and tests, commas and brackets will have the best stylistic effect.

KEY TAKEAWAY

A parenthesis is a word, or a group of words (phrase), inserted into a sentence to add information (explain or elaborate). It is between **a pair of brackets, commas or dashes**. When removed, the sentence still works on its own.

Parenthesis = explanation or extra information

 OVER TO YOU

As soon as Olivia starts writing, she loses attention and forgets what she wants to put down on paper. After Mrs Lee marked Olivia's essay, she wrote on the board, 'Writing clearly isn't easy.' She then turned to the class and declared: 'If any student can punctuate this sentence correctly, I'll give Olivia another chance to complete her work.'

Writing clearly isn't easy.

Luckily, after reading about Jake and Ella, you already know how to help Olivia.

Writing **(clearly)** isn't easy.

Writing**,** clearly**,** isn't easy.

Writing **–** clearly **–** isn't easy.

If you really want to impress Mrs Lee, change 'isn't' to 'is not' when using brackets and commas to show a more formal style of writing.

LEMON SQUEEZY

Olivia's friend is good at writing essays, but her handwriting is terrible. Teachers find it impossible to decipher most words. Can you help Olivia's friend punctuate the sentence to let her teacher know she is finding writing neatly difficult?

Writing clearly isn't easy.

If you've looked at the sentence and left it as it is – good job! This is probably the only time doing nothing gets you points.

The sentence says it as it is: writing clearly isn't easy.

STEP IT UP
Can you put in missing pairs of brackets, commas or dashes?
Reminder: dashes are best used in informal writing.

After I drank the water making an awkward gurgling noise I put the glass down forcefully.

Mrs Shirley who never cooked in her life was made the Head of Food Tech.

Zeenat finally turned around after looking away for two minutes and explained why the keys had disappeared.

I'll do this though I'm not promising if I get more free time.

I checked the clock the one on the city hall before getting on the bus.

Jason my only Instagram follower wouldn't do this to me!

I'll get back to you I hope tomorrow afternoon.

We are definitely coming in the summer more details soon so we get to meet Sophia in person.

Miss Rutherford paused at which point I shut my eyes before confirming I wasn't allowed to re-sit the test.

I looked in the suggested direction to the right of the post office but didn't see anything unusual.

If you have to comment we know you find it hard not to at least be fair.

Play is the most natural activity right after physiological functions and should be promoted by teachers and parents.

He didn't run so fast to win the race perish the thought though he can be competitive.

Being a young child is without any doubt whatsoever being a smaller human than an adult.

She was rather unfortunately the only candidate we had.

My dog's counting skills and I'm being absolutely honest here are superior to those of my cat.

The family holiday was all things considered a resounding success.

22

Ellipsis

After Katie hijacked every conversation at the dinner table, Dad decided to take action.

'Katie, you can't cut in every...'

'Daaad! It's not...'

'You've just...'

'Because I'm trying to...'

'You can't just... Katie!'

'I'm the football player of the week!'

'You...'

'Yes! I'm the football player of the week.'

'That's...'

'No one has listened since I got back from school. You all just talk and talk.'

'I'm...'

'That's okay, Dad. I'm off to the park.'

Dad walked across to the kitchen window and watched Katie ride off on her bike.

'Why didn't she say?' he wondered.

STOP AND THINK
More than half of the conversation between Katie and Dad ends in 'dot dot dots'. What's their exact effect? Why are they there?

The speakers (whether Katie or Dad) are not able to complete their speech because they're being interrupted.

OR TRYING TO SEND UNFINISHED SOS MESSAGES

I take your point, Zed. Dot dot dot is 'S' in the Morse code alphabet.

$$\cdot\cdot\cdot\ \_\ \_\ \_\ \cdot\cdot\cdot$$

S O S

KEY TAKEAWAY

The ellipsis (dot dot dot) shows that words have been left out.

This can be due to:
1. interruption (the speaker is not able to complete their speech),
2. the information is not relevant to the rest of the writing, or
3. to provide a pause, special effect or surprise ending.

(1) 'I don't think children of your age should**...**'

'But Daad!'

(2) 'Talking isn't doing**...** words are not deeds.' (Shakespeare)

Full quote: 'Talking isn't doing. It is a kind of good deed to say well; and yet words are not deeds.'

(3) When the clock strikes 13**...** it's time to get a new clock!

DID YOU KNOW?

The name 'ellipsis' comes from the ancient Greek word meaning 'omission' and 'to fall short'. That's how the punctuation mark has two purposes: to leave words out, and to create a special effect, for example a surprise ending or suspension.

OVER TO YOU

Can you find all places where the use of ellipsis would improve the sentences? Re-write them so they all have correct punctuation marks.

I like to hold hands at the movies but it always seems to startle strangers

. . . .

. . . .

I'm just going to flip this omelette Okay, we're having scrambled eggs

. . . .

. . . .

Your secret is safe with me I wasn't even listening

. . . .

. . . .

My friends and I played hide and seek It went on for hours Well, good friends are hard to find

. . . .

. . . .

My superpower is making people laugh which would be great if I were trying to be funny

. . . .

. . . .

I love my life but it just wants to be friends

. . . .

. . . .

A bus station is where a bus stops A train station is where a train stops On my desk I have a work station

. . . .

. . . .

23

Hyphen

When we put two or more words together to make a new word, we end up with a compound word.

Some compound words are open: there's a space between the two words, for example 'living room', 'coffee mug', 'dinner jacket'.

Others are closed: there's no space between them, for example 'bookmark', 'fireman', 'notebook'.

And then there are **hyphenated compounds**: there's a hyphen between the individual words, for example 'up-to-date', 'co-operate', 'two-year-old'.

WHY NOT HY-PHENATED

Because 'hy' and 'phenated' didn't exist as separate words before. I like your creativity, though.

When I was a teacher, I asked my class to use the word 'hyphenated' in a sentence. One student wrote, 'I would put a space between two words, but I can't because a hyphen ate it.' Another called the hyphen 'the most connected punctuation mark' with bodyguards (supporting words) glued to it on both sides.

SMARTY-PANTS STUDENTS ALERT

STOP AND THINK
How do we know when to put a hyphen in a compound word?

This can be tricky because the language is constantly changing. It's best to look up the word in an up-to-date dictionary. Many closed compound words started off as hyphenated ones. Not long ago, 'email' was 'e-mail', 'online' was 'on-line', and 'recycle' was 're-cycle'.

SO WHY BOTHER WITH HYPHENS

Hyphens prevent confusion during reading. Here's an example.

OVER TO YOU
Last month I worked 80 hours in school. Which of the three (almost identical) sentences is correctly hyphenated to reflect my total number of hours worked?

> 1. I did twenty four-hour shifts.
>
> 2. I did twenty-four hour shifts.
>
> 3. I did twenty-four-hour shifts.

If you've got the answer, can you match the remaining sentences to their correct numbers of hours?

> A. It's not possible to tell
>
> B. 24 hours
>
> C. 80 hours

STEP IT UP
Which of the sentences matches the description in bold?

He is 22 years old and sells old furniture.

✗_____ He is an old furniture salesman.

✓_____ He is an old-furniture salesman.

He is not very tall at all, and his job involves writing stories.

_____ He is a short-story writer.

_____ He is a short story writer.

She is a holiday rep who works from countries other than UK.

_____ She is an overseas holiday rep.

_____ She is an overseas-holiday rep.

In his 60s, he is an experienced cheese specialist.

_____ He is a mature cheese expert.

_____ He is a mature-cheese expert.

LEMON SQUEEZY

Can you match the pictures to the correct sentences?

(A)

---

1. It was a cross section of people.
2. It was a cross-section of people.

(B)

C

> 3. It was a man hunting beast.
>
> 4. It was a man-hunting beast.

D

KEY TAKEAWAY

A hyphen is shorter than a dash and there's no space on either side of it. It clings to the two words it is squeezed into.

The hyphen makes one (compound) word from two (connected) words:

A car that is light blue becomes **a light-blue car**.

Sometimes three or four connected words are easier to read when a hyphen is used:

Malia is **a happy-go-lucky girl**.

It is also used to make prefix and root words easier to read:

co-ordinate, re-educate, pre-school, ex-captain

 STEP IT UP

Can you re-write the sentences using hyphenated words?

Dad kissed his little girl good night.

Dad gave his little girl **a good-night kiss**.

. . . .

This grocery voucher is worth forty pounds.

. . . .

We never miss the parties at the end of term.

. . . .

This assignment is well thought out.

. . . .

My brother is nine years old.

. . . .

These clothes are made in a factory.

· ·

Airplanes that fly low create noise pollution.

· ·

The pattern on his top is eye catching.

· ·

BRING IT ON
Can you re-write the sentences so that there are no hyphens in them?

These people are **law-abiding citizens**.

These people are law abiding.
· ·

I wish she weren't such **a quick-tempered girl**.

· ·

What do you do when you meet **a well-known person**?

· ·

Many countries have **a 35-hour working week**.

· ·

I'm pleased to reveal **an up-to-date schedule**.

· ·

This is **a long-term solution**.

· ·

Unfortunately, he was described as **a short-fused politician**.

· ·

TAKE A BOW

Open, closed or hyphenated compounds? Use a dictionary to find the correct form and re-write the sentences.

A best friend is like a four leaf clover: hard to find and lucky to have.

. . . .

. . . .

Was the teacher cross eyed, or she simply couldn't control her pupils?

. . . .

. . . .

Waking up this morning was an eye opening experience.

. . . .

. . . .

Teachers who take class register are absent minded.

. . . .

. . . .

Whiteboards are quite re markable.

. . . .

. . . .

Auto correct should have been named more precisely as auto assume.

. . . .

. . . .

A key chain is a device that enables you to lose all keys at once.

. . . .

. . . .

The worst things about parallel parking are the eye witnesses.

· ·

· ·

If you spent your day in a well, can you say your day was well spent?

· ·

· ·

I was hoping to steal some left overs from the party, but I guess my plans were foiled.

· ·

· ·

Two Wi Fi antennas got married last Saturday. The reception was fantastic.

· ·

· ·

I've just been on a once in a lifetime holiday. I'll tell you what, never again!

· ·

· ·

I thought my neighbours were lovely people. Then they went and put a password on their Wi Fi.

· ·

· ·

What does a spy do in the rain? He goes under cover.

· ·

· ·

The short fortune teller who escaped from prison was a small medium at large.

· ·

· ·

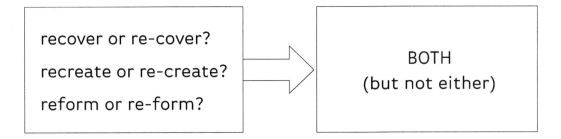

recover or re-cover?

recreate or re-create?

reform or re-form?

→ BOTH
(but not either)

 STOP AND THINK
How is it possible that some words are correct with and without a hyphen?

It depends on the word's meaning:

recover = get better when one is unwell

re-cover = cover something or someone again

OVER TO YOU
What do these words mean? It's not cheating if you use a dictionary.

recreate = ...

re-create = ...

reform = ...

re-form = ...

24

Inverted Commas

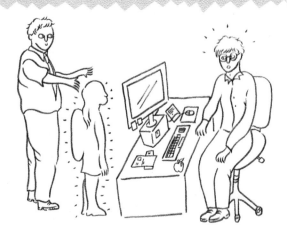

I'll be surprised if it gives you chills...

Mr Higgins is a busy headteacher. The school administrator has just made a record of their conversation about a Year 8 student. But which version, with single or double inverted commas, is correct?

> 'Mr Higgins, Johanna is waiting to speak to you. She says she feels invisible.'
> 'Oh dear. I can't see her right now.'

> "Mr Higgins, Johanna is waiting to speak to you. She says she feels invisible."
> "Oh dear. I can't see her right now."

Either is correct, as long as you don't change your speech marks (or quotation marks) from single to double (or the other way round) in the same piece of writing.

STOP AND THINK
What's the difference between 'inverted commas', 'speech marks' and 'quotation marks'? They all look the same.

'Inverted commas' is a term used for both 'speech marks' and 'quotation marks'. Although they look the same, there are a few differences.

Speech marks are used when people are actually speaking. Their words are called **direct speech**. You'll see a lot of direct speech in novels, stories and any writing with dialogue in it.

The punctuation mark at the end of direct speech is always **inside the second set of speech marks**. This is so we capture everything said by someone, including the punctuation mark that ends the direct speech.

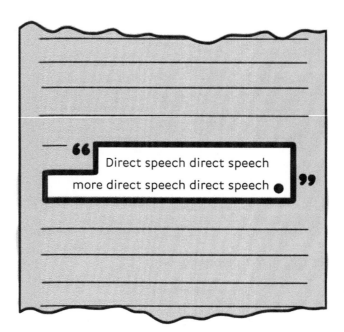

 "I'm in glove with you," said the finger to the thumb.

 "I'm in glove with you", said the finger to the thumb.

 I said to myself, 'I can't believe that cloning machine has worked!'

 I said to myself, 'I can't believe that cloning machine has worked'!

Quotation marks show that we are quoting what someone has said, or referring to something that was stated by someone else.

Here, the focus is on both the sentence itself and the quoted words within the sentence. The final punctuation mark (for example, a full stop or comma) is part of the whole sentence and is **outside the second set of quotation marks**.

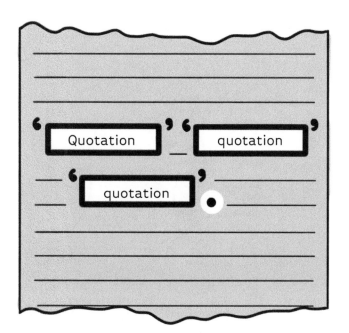

 As he stood outside, he told us to call him 'outstanding'.

 As he stood outside, he told us to call him 'outstanding.'

 "Running a half marathon" sounds so much better than "quitting halfway through a marathon".

 "Running a half marathon" sounds so much better than "quitting halfway through a marathon."

STOP AND DECIDE
Rob was close to thinking that Annie was playing Chinese Whispers.
Are both reports from Rob and Annie correctly punctuated?

I heard Annie whisper, **"**Any big turtles you had to overcome on your trip to Antarctica**?"**

I whispered to Rob, **"**Any big hurdles you had to overcome on your trip to Antarctica**"?**

Rob's statement (first box) is correctly punctuated, but Annie's (second box) isn't. Both sentences include direct speech (what they actually said).

As is the case with all punctuation marks, it's not enough to use them – it's more important to use them **in the right place** in the sentence.

OVER TO YOU
Can you match the pictures to the correct sentences?

 A

1. The policeman said, "The robber was too quick."

2. "The policeman," said the robber, "was too quick."

B

KEY TAKEAWAY

Inverted commas are used to show the reader the exact place where direct speech or quotation begins and ends.

Direct speech is what someone says 'word for word' – this can be a sentence, or a few sentences. The punctuation mark at the end of direct speech is always **inside the second set of speech marks**.

Quotation takes place when we are quoting what someone has said, or referring to something that was stated by someone else. The final punctuation mark is **outside** the second set of quotation marks.

LEMON SQUEEZY
Can you insert all missing inverted commas? They can be single or double, but be consistent when using them in the same sentence or passage.

My neighbour used to say, As one door closes, another opens. Such a lovely man, but a terrible cabinet maker.

Dogs are easily amused, thought Sam while watching her dog chase his tail. She then realised that she was watching her dog chase his tail.

I put the pro in procrastinate.

Don't spell part backwards – it's a trap!

Whoever invented Knock knock jokes should get a No bell prize.

When you just slipped and fell, simply say, Yep, gravity still works!

I'm all for irony, but the phrase Good morning is proving a bit too far.

Pool rule: you're not allowed to do anything that begins with the words: Hey everyone, watch this!

Does anyone actually know what the I'm feeling lucky button on the Google page means?

Most of the year: I want this, I want that! Near my birthday: I can't think of a single thing I want.

Teachers use words such as creative and strong-willed to describe Esme. We simply think she is stubborn.

If you send a text message saying, I heard what you said about me, you could find out rather a lot about what the person thinks about you.

Did you know that if you hold your ear up to a stranger's knee, you can actually hear them say, What do you think you are doing?

Sometimes, when I am matching socks, I'm horrified to think, What if these two socks don't even like each other?

I saw a doctor about my hearing problem. He asked, Can you describe the symptoms? I said, Homer is fat, Marge has blue hair, Maggie has the brains and Bart is a real nightmare.

I like to give people blank Thank you cards for their birthdays. When they ask me what they're for, I say, You'll thank me later!

Doctor: Sir, I'm afraid your DNA is backwards. Me: And?

People used to laugh at me when I would announce, I want to be a comedian! Well, nobody's laughing now.

I got my sister a Get better soon card. She's not sick – I just think she could get better.

Maggie pleaded, Please eat the broken biscuits first because I feel so bad for them.

Dads everywhere: Don't worry, kids. Mum just turned the car radio down, so we shouldn't be lost much longer.

What's an essay conclusion, Jamie?
That part where you're tired of thinking.

Text to Mum: I'll be there in 5 minutes. If not, read this message again.

I was complimented on my fine driving. Someone left a Parking Fine note.

A man went to the doctor's and said, I've hurt my arm in several places. The doctor said, Well, don't go there any more.

Teacher: You missed school yesterday.
Joe: To tell you the truth, I didn't really miss it.

I read recipes the same way I read sci-fi stories: I get to the end and think, Well, that's not going to happen!

25
Possessive Apostrophe

Apostrophes are used to show possession – something **belongs** to someone or something. And when something belongs, there is **an owner**.

The 'owner' word is the one that has an apostrophe and a letter 's' attached to them.

But let's not get ahead of ourselves... Let's start with a story.

Ali's teacher asked the class to write a list of best qualities that people closest to them possessed. Now, Ali is the class comedian – she wouldn't simply write a list of lovely adjectives: she wrote a story she knew everyone would find hilarious.

'Dads jokes are as dull as his socks,' started Ali. 'And his socks are always grey.' She then laughed into her sleeve so much that the teacher asked her to be the first one to share her list with the class.

Ali composed herself and read her work, but no one laughed. The whole class stared at the teacher's grey socks, occasionally looking up at his pale face with a faint smile. You've guessed it: Ali's father is the class teacher.

OVER TO YOU
Look at Ali's sentence below and help her decide where to place an apostrophe. Does it go with 'Dads' or 'jokes'? Both words have an 's' at the end, but Ali is not sure which one has a missing apostrophe.

Dads jokes are as dull as his socks.

Start by finding the 'owner' word. Whose jokes are they? Who 'owns' the jokes?

Dad.

Now use your thumbs to cover all the words apart from 'Dad' because it's the owner word.

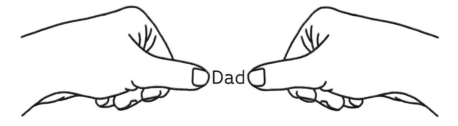

Your right thumbnail shows you where the apostrophe should go.

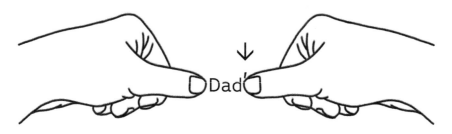

Now the sentence has an apostrophe in the right place.

> Dad's jokes are as dull as his socks.

Imagine a few other children in Ali's class said the same about their fathers.

> Dads jokes are as dull as **their** socks.

Where does the apostrophe go if the word (Dads) is plural?

We do exactly as we did before using our thumbs.

Who owns the jokes? Dads.

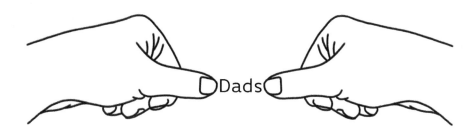

And where does the apostrophe go? Where your right thumbnail is.

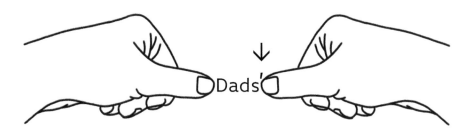

Dads' jokes are as dull as **their** socks.

If you do this to all 'owner' words, you'll always know where the apostrophe goes. Let's try again. Copy this sentence:

Some peoples pets look like them.

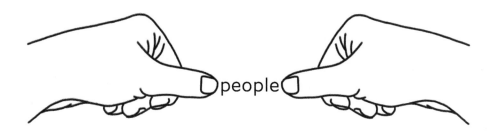

Now put the apostrophe where your right thumbnail is.

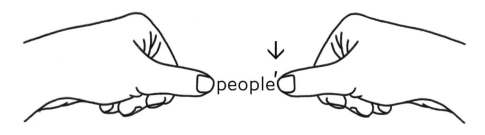

And here is the sentence:

✓ Some people's pets look like them.

Great job. I've got one more example to show you. Copy the sentence below. We need to do something with the three 's's in a row!

The princesss hand had six fingers.

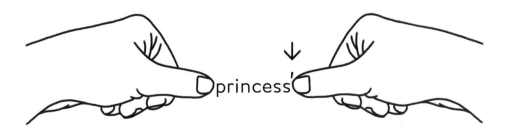

✓ The princess's hand had six fingers.

 STOP AND THINK
Does the ending -ss's look odd to you?

Some writers drop the last 's'. You'll see **princess' hand** instead of **princess's hand**. Or **James' school** instead of **James's school**. For us, it's best to stick to our thumbs method and all the '-s's and '-ss's that go with it because you can never go wrong with it.

So, yes, princess's hand is correct. So is James's school.

A FRIENDLY REMINDER I HAVE NO THUMBS

Luckily, your visual search is superior to the nimblest of thumbs.

KEY TAKEAWAY

Apostrophes are used to show possession – something **belongs** to someone or something. And when something belongs, there is an **owner**.

The 'owner' word is the one that has an apostrophe and a letter 's' attached to them.

The apostrophe can be before or after the added letter 's'. It is before the 's' if it's a singular noun (a boy's bike), and after the 's' if it's a plural one (boys' bikes).

Be sure to never use an apostrophe to make a word plural!

✓ Teas and coffees are served here.

✗ Tea**'s** and coffee**'s** are served here.

 BREEZE THROUGH

Place your thumbs on top of 'owner' words to decide where to put missing apostrophes. Do all sentences have missing apostrophes?

Mums stories are very funny, but not when she jokes about Pebbles first encounter with the vet.

Windows are really TVs for cats.

If you step on someones foot, they open their mouth like a bin.

From the chairs viewpoint, humans are mainly bums.

Which countrys capital is the fastest growing? Irelands. Every year it's Dublin.

These are childrens books; dictionaries are over there.

Mollys dream was to never have spinach flan ever again.

I have two baby sisters and the babies cots are right next to my bed.

Mens coats are to your left, and womens shoes are on the first floor.

Mr Spark was asked to park in the visitors car park.

Dads bosss pen was in his pocket.

We could ask Adams brother to babysit for us.

If you want to stop an astronauts baby from crying, you rocket.

A vampires favourite fruit is obviously a blood orange.

Mr Normans message on the schools website: 'To the student who stole my glasses. I will find you. I have contacts.'

How many musicians does it take to screw in a lightbulb? And a one, and a two, and a three...

You can tell an ants gender by putting it in water: sinks – girl ant, floats – buoyant.

 **BRING IT ON**

These signs have been displayed without checking for correct punctuation. Can you help their writers correct all punctuation errors?

THOMPSONS BAKERY

No barbeque's allowed on the field

NO TAXI'S RESIDENT'S CARS ONLY

Hot drink's served here

NOTICE
Toilet's to the right

CARS PARKED AT OWNERS RISK

St Mary's Childrens Hospital

26

Contracting Apostrophe

Did you hear about Colin, the grammar police officer? A master of distractions and rubbish at contractions (shortened words). Colin couldn't remember whether his line was 'Your under arrest' or 'You're under arrest'. After he lost his job, he thought, 'Who's job was it, anyway?' He then corrected himself, 'Whose job was it, anyway?' Poor, confused Colin. He put his hand on top of his head and whispered to the mirror, 'Their, they're, there...'

You're under arrest**!**

Worry not, Colin. If you have a piece of paper and a paper clip to hand, you can make your very own word contraction device. The paper clip will be your apostrophe.

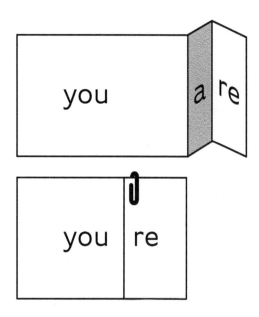

you're is short for **you are**

your is a possessive determiner like **his, her** or **their**
your means **belonging to you**

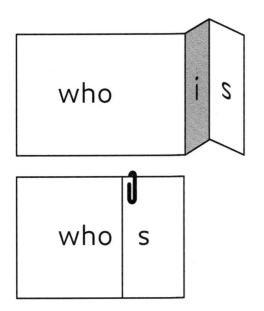

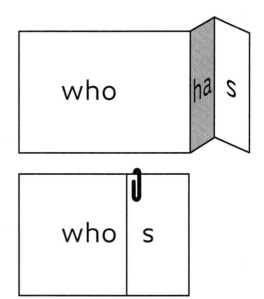

OVER TO YOU

who's is short for . . . . or . . . .

. . . .

whose is asking '**Who does this** . . . .?'

APOSTROPHE FACTS

Words that have apostrophes in place of missing letters are called **contractions**. They contract, or become shorter.

Note the difference between **its** = belonging to it (a possessive determiner like **his**, **her** or **their**) and **it's** = **it is** or **it has**

The cat licked its paw.
Where's the key? I think **it's** on the table.

Don't write **would of** or **should of** when you mean **would've** = **would have**, or **should've** = **should have**.
The former ones are incorrect.

✗ You **shouldn't of**, really. I **would of** done it myself.

✓ You **shouldn't have**, really. I **would've** done it myself.

BREEZE THROUGH

Fun time! It's your turn to get a piece of paper and a paper clip, and make your word contraction device. Start with the phrases below. What contractions did you get?

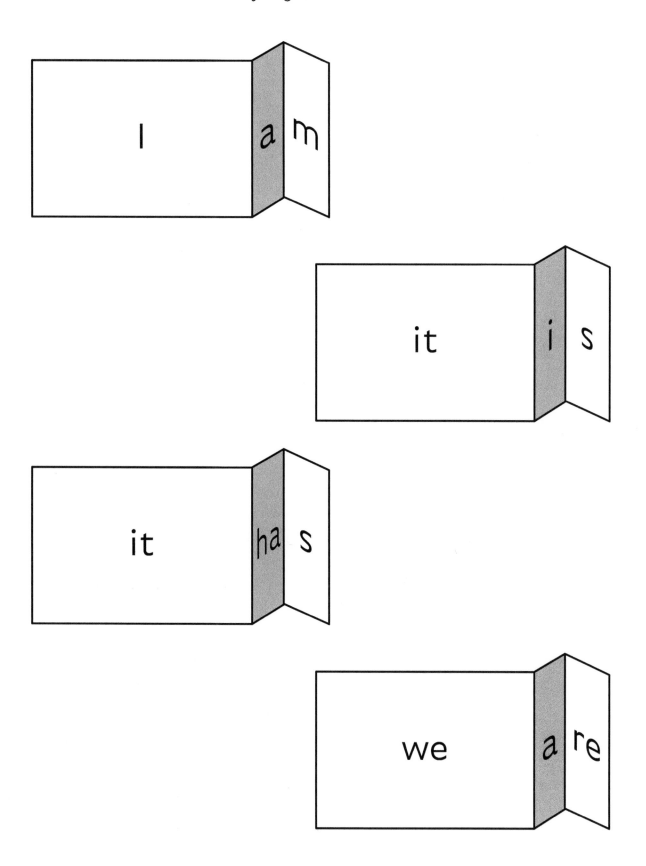

LEMON SQUEEZY

What missing letters are hidden in these contractions?
Remember the paper clip is your apostrophe.

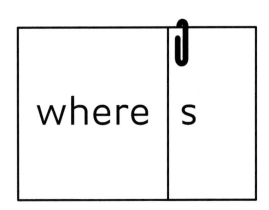

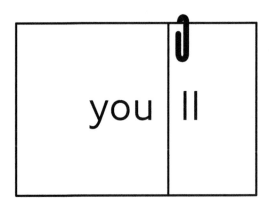

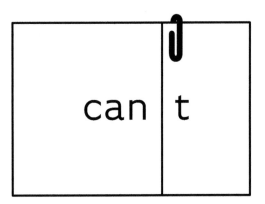

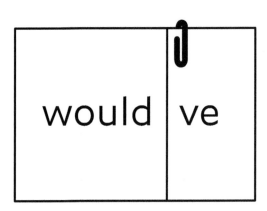

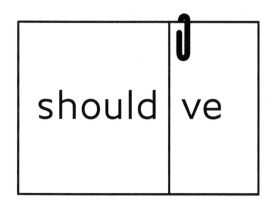

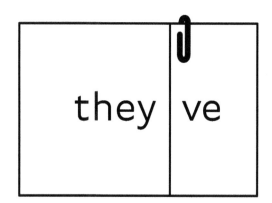

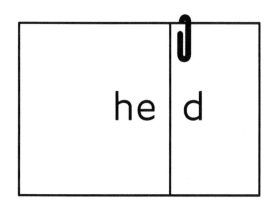

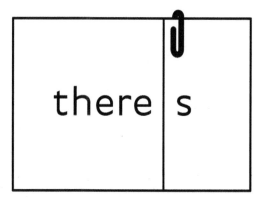

WHAT IS 'O'CLOCK' SHORT FOR?

The first mechanical clock was invented in the 14th century, although clocks remained relatively rare even in the 16th century. People would refer to the position of the sun during the day, and the moon at night. Not surprisingly, their time-telling skills lacked accuracy.

In those days, when someone referred to the time provided by an actual clock (as opposed to any other method), they would say 'of the clock', for example 'Four of the clock'. In time, the phrase became shortened to 'o'clock'.

ALERT IN MY DATA ANALYSIS

THE FOLDING DEVICE DOESNT WORK FOR ALL CONTRACTIONS

You know what's causing the problem, don't you? The most negative word in the world.

NO WIFI

That's two words, Zed! Though the first one is close enough.

The word 'not' doesn't contract in the usual way. The middle 'o' is missing, so our paper folding method needs updating to include a different folding pattern.

 BRING IT ON
Your challenge is to experiment with different folding methods until you can demonstrate how these contractions work:

is **not** = is**n't** ⁣⁣ was **not** = was**n't**
are **not** = are**n't** ⁣⁣ were **not** = were**n't**
will **not** = w**on't** ⁣⁣ have **not** = have**n't**
shall **not** = sha**n't** ⁣⁣ has **not** = has**n't**
would **not** = would**n't** ⁣⁣ had **not** = had**n't**
could **not** = could**n't** ⁣⁣ do **not** = do**n't**
should **not** = should**n't** ⁣⁣ does **not** = does**n't**
must **not** = must**n't** ⁣⁣ did **not** = did**n't**

CHALLENGE ACCEPTED

I didn't mean you, Zed. You said you had no thumbs, remember?

BREEZE THROUGH
Now complete the list from memory.

it's	=	it is, or it has
I'm	=	. . . .
you'll	=	. . . .
wasn't	=	. . . .
could've	=	. . . .
we're	=	. . . .
they've	=	. . . .
can't	=	. . . .
mustn't	=	. . . .
he'd	=	. . . .
aren't	=	. . . .
hadn't	=	. . . .
wouldn't	=	. . . .
should've	=	. . . .
won't	=	. . . .
might've	=	. . . .
shan't	=	. . . .
they're	=	. . . .
who's	=	. . . .
hasn't	=	. . . .
there's	=	. . . .
couldn't	=	. . . .
weren't	=	. . . .
didn't	=	. . . .

KEY TAKEAWAY

Apostrophes are used to shorten words by removing one or more letters. The shortened words are known as **contractions**.

We use contractions in spoken English and informal written English. They make communication more efficient, as contractions are easier to pronounce.

 STOP AND COMPARE
A missing apostrophe can change the meaning of some words.

she'll or **shell?**
we're or **were?**
she'd or **shed?**
we'll or **well?**

 STOP AND THINK
How can you tell when an apostrophe is needed and when it is not?

Start by assuming that the word is a contraction, 'unfold' it and say it in full, then check if the sentence still makes sense. Let's try these examples:

We'll (we will) be happy to meet you by the **well**.

Where **were** you last night? I was looking for you to tell you **we're (we are)** away tomorrow?

After **she'd (she had)** seen the burglars caught in the **shed**, she didn't **shed** a single tear.

She'll (she will) be so happy with that **shell** you found on the beach.

 STEP IT UP
This task has tongue twisters and punctuation problems in one. Can you put in all missing contracting apostrophes?

Shell sell a shell by the seashore.
The shell shell sell will be very well wrapped.

Were aware that you were away.
Were we not aware youre away, we wouldnt worry were on our own.

The shed shed bought needed some shade.
Shed better get the shed that shed planned to buy.

Well write to you about the well well in time.
Dont change the price, or well change our mind about the well.

 TAKE A BOW
Can you add all missing apostrophes? Write out the contractions in full in brackets.

It's (It is) a 30-minute walk from my house to the school, but a 10-minute walk back home. **I'd (I would)** say **it's (it is)** a mystery!

Ive had a row with my boss at lunchtime – one of the perks of working near a boating lake.

. . . .

. . . .

Its so annoying when people get their sayings wrong. After all, its not rocket salad!

. . . .

. . . .

No matter how enraged Germaine Greer gets, shell never be as furious as her sister, Anne.

. . . .

. . . .

Finding my lost luggage at the airport is a nightmare. You might think itd be easy, but thats not the case.

. . . .

. . . .

My boyfriend found a pile of letters Id hidden and accused me of cheating. He said hed never play scrabble with me again.

. . . .

. . . .

Ive done my first ever book signing. Im now banned from the library.

. . . .

. . . .

I dont see the point of a pocket calculator. Who doesnt know how many pockets they have?

. . . .

. . . .

Whos in charge of the hankies? The handkerchief.

. . . .

. . . .

Id bought rocket salad but it's gone off before I could eat it.

. . . .

. . . .

To be Frank, Id have to change my name.

. . . .

. . . .

Hes quit his job at the helium factory today. Hes not being spoken to in that tone of voice!

. . . .

. . . .

27

How to Solve a Problem like Zed?

Zed, Zed! We've got it!

GOT WHAT

Your punctuation software update. I can't wait to listen to you read books!

ID RATHER HAVE A ZILLION SYSTEM BUGS THAN SOUND LIKE ALEXA

Hang on. Someone's tampered with the activation key. Zed, have...?

THREAT DETECTED EVACUATE EVACUATE EVACUATE

OVER TO YOU
Can you help me recover the activation key to show Zed that punctuation is nothing to worry about?

Work through the sequence of sentences and decide which one is correctly punctuated (there'll only be one per set). Record your answer to the right of the set, as it's part of the key.

Good luck!

START HERE

ACTIVATION KEY CHARACTER 1

(A) When I close my eyes I can't see.

(V) When I close my eyes I cant see.

(W) **When I close my eyes, I can't see.**

(E) When I close my eyes; I can't see.

CORRECT ANSWER

(W)

ACTIVATION KEY CHARACTER 2

(I) I could've done it if I'd tried harder.

(L) I could of done it, if I'd tried harder.

(B) I could've done it, if I tried harder.

(W) I could of done it if I tried harder.

CORRECT ANSWER

( )

ACTIVATION KEY CHARACTER 3

(D) Ollie's brother's choice was to sell their shares in the company.

(N) Ollie's brothers' choice was to sell their shares in the company.

(S) Ollies' brothers' choice was to sell their shares in the company.

(E) Ollie's brothers' choice was to sell their shares' in the company.

CORRECT ANSWER

( )

ACTIVATION KEY CHARACTER 4

(N) It's not true all of our teachers' worries are students' grades.

(E) Its not true all of our teachers' worry's are students' grades.

(I) It's not true all of our teacher's worries are student's grades.

(A) It's not true all of our teacher's worries are student's grade's.

CORRECT ANSWER

( )

ACTIVATION KEY CHARACTER 5

(P) Tolkien famously said, "Not all those who wander are lost".

(K) Tolkien famously said, 'Not all those who wander are lost."

(I) Tolkien famously said, "Not all those who wander are lost."

(M) Tolkien famously said "Not all those who wander are lost.'

CORRECT ANSWER

ACTIVATION KEY CHARACTER 6

(Y) Having played in manchester the band is coming to our city.

(N) Having played in Manchester, the band is coming to our city.

(C) Having played in Manchester the band is coming to our city.

(N) Having played in Manchester – the band is coming to our city.

CORRECT ANSWER

ACTIVATION KEY CHARACTER 7

(Z) The team struggled to communicate, we lost the game.

(T) The team struggled to communicate: We lost the game.

(E) The team struggled to communicate – We lost the game.

(G) The team struggled to communicate; we lost the game.

CORRECT ANSWER

ACTIVATION KEY CHARACTER 8

(H) I'm off, Lily. Please feed Scratch, Clawsby, Catzilla and Pud.

(O) I'm off Lily. Please feed Scratch, Clawsby, Catzilla and Pud.

(M) I'm off, Lily. Please feed Scratch, Clawsby, Catzilla and, Pud.

(F) I'm off Lily; please feed scratch, clawsby, catzilla and pud.

CORRECT ANSWER

ACTIVATION KEY CHARACTER 9

(A) Just as I finished, it started raining, which ruined my project.

(N) Just as I finished it started raining, which ruined my project.

(R) Just as I finished, it started raining which ruined my project.

(C) Just as I finished; it started raining, which ruined my project.

CORRECT
ANSWER

ACTIVATION KEY CHARACTER 10

(G) Children's party's are welcome here.

(N) Children's parties are welcome here.

(A) Childrens' parties are welcome here.

(D) Children's partys' are welcome here.

CORRECT
ANSWER

ACTIVATION KEY CHARACTER 11

(J) The full amount – first requested in June – is yet to be paid.

(D) The full amount, first requested in June, is yet to be paid.

(Q) The full amount; first requested in June; is yet to be paid.

(Y) The full amount (First requested in June) is yet to be paid.

CORRECT
ANSWER

ACTIVATION KEY CHARACTER 12

(R) With the exception of one hiccup – the lesson went rather well.

(L) With the exception of one hiccup; the lesson went rather well.

(B) With the exception of one hiccup: the lesson went rather well.

(S) With the exception of one hiccup, the lesson went rather well.

CORRECT
ANSWER

ACTIVATION KEY CHARACTER 13

(G) The new teacher, that looks like Doctor Who, is our form tutor.

(D) The new teacher, who looks like Doctor Who, is our form tutor.

(A) The new teacher who looks like Doctor Who is our form tutor.

(T) The new teacher; that looks like Doctor Who; is our form tutor.

CORRECT ANSWER

ACTIVATION KEY CHARACTER 14

(U) According to Mr Frost, the students worked 'exceptionally hard.'

(O) According to Mr Frost, the students worked 'exceptionally hard'.

(S) According to Mr Frost, the students worked "exceptionally hard."

(B) According to Mr Frost the students worked 'exceptionally hard'.

CORRECT ANSWER

ACTIVATION KEY CHARACTER 15

(W) Who's left their jacket behind?

(D) Whose left their jacket behind?

(B) Who'se left their jacket behind?

(F) Whose left their jacked behind!

CORRECT ANSWER

ACTIVATION KEY CHARACTER 16

(M) Jo's second hand car theft account seemed a far-fetched story.

(E) Jo's second-hand car theft account seemed a far fetched story.

(J) Jo's second hand car theft account seemed a far fetched story.

(N) Jo's second-hand car theft account seemed a far-fetched story.

CORRECT ANSWER

COMPLETED ACTIVATION KEY

1	2	3	4	5	6	7	8	9	10	11	12	13	14	15	16
W															

Have you got the correct key to activate Zed's punctuation software update? Compare it with the key on the first page of the next section. (It'll help if you look closely at Zed's image.)

 BRING IT ON

If you've had fun completing the above exercise, you will enjoy helping Zed re-visit all the things it had said in this book prior to its punctuation software update. You'll remember its expressions look like this:

THANKS FOR HELPING BILLY GET OUT OF THE HOUSE

But we want them to have punctuation marks and look like this:

Thanks for helping, Billy. Get out of the house!

And like this:

Is 'Star Wars' a title or a brand name? Asking for R2-D2...

Are you in? Zed will be thrilled!

28

Zed Has the Last Word

Nearly every chapter in this book reminded you to carefully check where you've placed a punctuation mark because it could change the sentence's meaning. You'll be relieved to know that there are sentences that are simply ambiguous whether we use punctuation marks or not. Remember, you've heard it from me first.

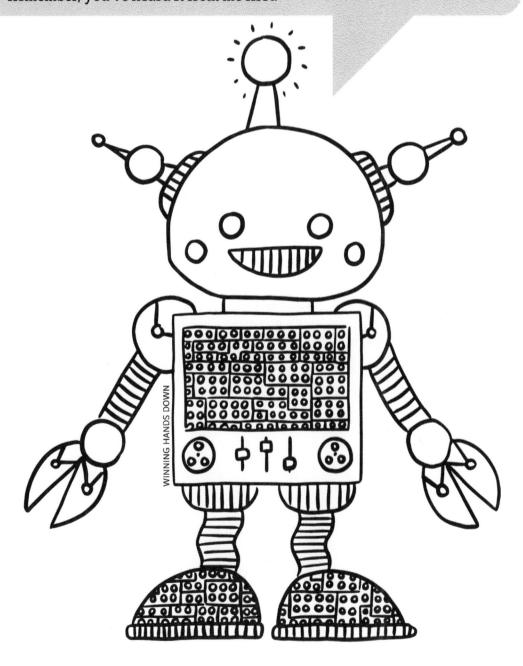

WINNING HANDS DOWN

OVER TO YOU

Can you work out the double meaning of these sentences?

The dog chased a man on a bicycle.
I saw her duck.
Free whales!
Look at the cat with one eye.
I saw the man with the telescope.
The vicar married my niece.
They fed her rat poison.
Visiting relatives can be boring.
He loves the hamster more than his wife.
The puppy sat by the girl with the pleased look.
Call me a taxi.
Giant waves down Queen Mary's funnels.

Answer Key

1. Why We Need Punctuation

OVER TO YOU

The three punctuation marks that can be placed at the end of a sentence (not all at once) are **the full stop**, **question mark** and **exclamation mark**. It is also possible for the second set of inverted commas (speech marks) and brackets to appear at the very end of a sentence, but you don't need to think about this until you start reading Chapter 24: Inverted Commas and Chapter 20: Brackets.

This pizza pie chart shows how frequently different punctuation marks appear in English texts.

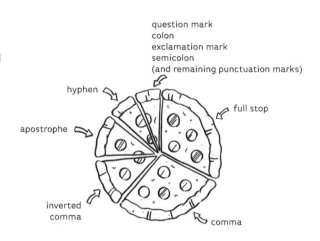

In 2013, researchers from Newcastle University (led by Professor Vivian Cook) scanned three novels, two newspapers, one business report and a few research papers, which combined contained 459,000 words. They then calculated the percentage of time the different punctuation marks appeared in the texts. I've created a table to show you their results:

full stop	31%
comma	29%
inverted comma	13%
apostrophe	12%
hyphen	7%
question mark	3%
colon	2%
exclamation mark	2%
semicolon (and remaining punctuation marks)	1%

2. Capital Letter

OVER TO YOU

Three missing capital letters:
'Two mysterious people live in my house: Somebody and Nobody. Somebody did it and Nobody knows who.'

This is a play-on-words joke: the common nouns 'somebody' and 'nobody' become proper nouns (people's names).

LEMON SQUEEZY

Dad didn't want every Tom, Dick and Harry using our front garden bench.

Rob Slater is training for the Winter Olympics.

The Queen will deliver a speech at the House of Lords.

When in Rome, do as the Romans do.

An Englishman's home is his castle.

Year 6 mums and dads waited outside the National Gallery in London.

Would you rather have a house in the Big Apple or Silicon Valley?

If the mountain will not come to Mahomet, Mahomet must go to the mountain.

Liz Chang, a Panorama journalist, reported live from Westminster.

Please, two more minutes, Dad. I'm not ready yet.

If Cinderella's shoe fit perfectly, then why did it fall off?

STEP IT UP
My brother bought two goldfish and named them One and Two.

If one dies, he'll still have two.

My brother won't have two fish, but he'll have the fish named Two.

'Can I have a bookmark?'
'My name is Mick.'
The second person heard, 'Can I have a book, Mark?'

I named my dog Five Miles so I can tell people that I walk five miles every day.

The phrase 'five miles' became a proper name after the first letters were capitalised.

I see no end, have no control and no home anymore.

I think it's time for a new keyboard.

Keyboard keys start with capital letters: End, Control, Home.

I used to be in a band called Lost Dog.

You probably saw our posters.

Titles in posters and notices are written in capital letters. 'Lost Dog' notices are more common than band posters.

I WRITE ALL MY JOKES IN CAPITALS.
THIS ONE WAS WRITTEN IN BERLIN.

When we say 'capitals' for 'capital letters', we mean 'upper case letters'.

STOP AND CHECK
I know a human as mad as a March hare.

BREEZE THROUGH
If Mondays were shoes, they wouldn't walk very far.

Mrs Ford always says Tuesday is just Monday's ugly sister.

Can February march? No, but April may.

Why are solders tired in April? They've had a long march. *(tired from marching)*

Why are solders tired in April? They've had a long March. *(tired of waiting for March to end)*

Did you know that May is the shortest month? It only has three letters.

Thirty days has September, April, June and November...

LEMON SQUEEZY
When the English language gets in my way, I create its next chapter.

The politician's speech is all double Dutch to me.

There's an Iranian proverb that says, 'Arabic is a language, Persian is a delicacy and Turkish is an art.'

When I speak German in class, there's no hiding place.

Did Julius Caesar speak Roman or Latin?

The English language is a child of German and French that was raised by the Vikings.

OVER TO YOU

We asked the hairdresser whether it's called the French plait or French braid.

The class played Chinese Whispers all morning.

Scientists believe the Western world plays Russian roulette with antibiotics.

Autumn heatwaves are called Indian summers.

We always have Peking duck and Cantonese soup in this restaurant.

Every time we shop for furniture, we end up having Swedish meatballs.

I'd love to know how the Earth rotates; it would surely make my day.

STEP IT UP

A group of Northern European countries that includes Denmark, Norway and Sweden is called **Scandinavia**. The people who live there are **Scandinavians**.

Some people think that Poland is in Eastern Europe; others believe that it's part of Central Europe. That makes the Poles either **Eastern Europeans** or **Central Europeans**.

The ethnic group of Americans whose ancestors came from Africa are called **African Americans**.

Mexico, Central America and most of South America where Spanish is the primary language were once under Spanish rule. Their cultures are referred to as **Hispanic** cultures.

LEMON SQUEEZY

Q: Why were the early days of history called the Dark Ages?

A: Because there were so many knights!

Q: How was the Roman Empire cut in half?

A: With a pair of Caesars!

Q: How did the Vikings send secret messages?

A: By Norse code!

(the Norse is the term for Medieval Norwegians or Scandinavians)

Q: What comes after the Bronze Age and the Iron Age?

A: The Heavy Metal age, Sir.

Q: Where did the Medieval King John sign the Magna Carta?

A: At the bottom.

STEP IT UP

The Festival of Lights and the Feast of Dedication are two other names for a Jewish holiday that is observed for eight days and nights, and is called **Hanukkah**.

Hanging stockings out comes from the Dutch custom of leaving shoes packed with food for St Nicholas's donkeys. St Nicholas would leave small gifts in return. This religious festival is called **Christmas**.

Diwali is an important religious festival in India celebrated between October and November. People often think of it as a Hindu festival, but it is also celebrated by Sikhs and Jains.

Chinese New Year starts a new animal's zodiac year. In China, each lunar cycle has 60 years and 12 years is regarded as a small cycle. Each of the 12 years is defined by an animal sign. 2020 is the Year of the Rat and 2021 is the Year of the Ox.

Easter, a Christian holiday, celebrates the resurrection of Jesus Christ. During Holy Week, Holy Thursday commemorates the time when the last supper was held. Good Friday commemorates Jesus's crucifixion and death.

During **Ramadan**, which lasts a month, Muslims don't eat or drink between dawn and sunset. Fasting helps them devote themselves to their faith and get closer to Allah. It is one of the Five Pillars of Islam, which form the basis of how Muslims live their lives.

The word 'carol' means dance or song of praise and joy. Carols used to be sung during all four seasons, but the tradition of singing them at **Christmas** is the only one to survive.

LEMON SQUEEZY

I just got hit on the head with a power tool. I was sitting there minding my own business, the next thing I know, Bosch!

Samsung, iPhone or Motorola – I can't picture myself without a camera phone.

Honestly, ice hockey is just a bunch of people fighting for the last Oreo.

If Apple built a house, would it have Windows?

I just stepped on some Cheerios on the floor. You can call me a cereal killer!

Why did the yellow M&M go to school? Because it wanted to be a Smartie.

There's a new a travel guide highlighting towns and cities with badly laid paving slabs. It's called TripAdvisor!

I thought I'd use my Tesco Clubcard to scrape the ice off my windscreen, but I could only get 10% off.

STEP IT UP

ICT – Information and Communication Technologies

AKA – also known as

DIY – do it yourself

FAQ – frequently asked questions

ETA – estimated time of arrival

BAFTA – British Academy of Film and Television Arts

RSVP – from French 'répondez s'il vous plait', which means 'please respond'

DOB – date of birth

RSPCA – Royal Society for the Prevention of Cruelty to Animals

NATO – North Atlantic Treaty Organisation

LGBT – lesbian, gay, bisexual and transgender

PTO – please turn over

NHS – National Health Service

MMXIX is 2019, MMXX is 2020, and MMXXIII is 2023.

TAKE A BOW

I = 1

MIX = 1009

CC = 200

CD = 400

CV = 105

DC = 600

MC = 1100

MD = 1500

LIV = 54

DI = 501

3. Full Stop

BREEZE THROUGH

Everything is funnier when you are not allowed to laugh.

My first name is Joe. My surname is Brown.

It's easier to pull than to push. It's also easier to sit than to stand.

Every class has one really funny student.

Dan bought chicken and Eastern spice. He is a fan of Moroccan kebabs.

I am told I am too cool for school.

Chocolate is God's apology for broccoli.

I didn't know Ankara was the capital of Turkey.

STEP IT UP

It's not true he wrote the letter. (*he didn't write the letter*)

It's not true. He wrote the letter. (*the truth is that he wrote the letter*)

Easy does it.

That was easy. Does it mean I can do it myself from now on?

It was true love.

It was true. Love struck Ahmed at the very moment he looked at Rabia.

We are trying to speak perfect French.

We are trying. To speak perfect French is to learn to roll your 'r's.

I don't know Katie. (*I don't know the girl called Katie*)

I don't know. Katie might. (*Katie might know the answer*)

We are friends forever.

We are friends. Forever seems shorter now.

OVER TO YOU

Sorry I'm late. I didn't want to come.

Ryan took a ruler to bed. He was upset it didn't say how long he slept.

Cinderella didn't make it to the football team. She ran away from the ball.

Dad's job is super confidential. He really hasn't got a clue what he's doing.

Some people say I'm lazy. I say I'm on energy saving mode.

Love is in the air. I'm going to wear my gas mask.

Fruit is 90% water. It is also 100% not pizza.

My teacher asked me to name all chemicals in the periodic table. I thought they already had names.

TAKE A BOW

I decided to clone myself. I thought I could send my clone to school while I stayed at home and played computer games. It obviously had to be a secret. I swore my cat Gremlin not to utter a single meow to anyone. I saw Dr Frankenbrain in the school lab and explained I needed to finish my old chemistry project. He let Gremlin be my guinea pig so long as he behaved himself. All was going well until Gremlin spotted a red dot on the cloning machine's controls and went mad chasing the light as well as its reflection on the wall. Dr Frankenbrain jumped in to help me manage the silly cat. The move was a disaster, as the place was full of fragile instruments and dangerous equipment. What I didn't know was that my teacher was really clumsy. He tripped over a cable and got zapped by the revving machine. Although he didn't get cloned, he became one fortieth of his normal size. He was much smaller than Gremlin.

I asked Dr Frankenbrain what I should do to get him back to his normal size. All I got back was a series of high-pitched squeaks. Gremlin the mad mice chaser did not wait for an invitation. He pounced on Dr Frankenbrain and ate him up in three superfast gulps. A shame really because I couldn't think of anyone else who could help me clone myself. As I was tidying up the lab, Gremlin gave out the loudest burp I've ever heard, which actually turned out to be my teacher's real voice...

4. Exclamation Mark

LEMON SQUEEZY

That mini heart attack you get when your foot slides down the stairs!

Stop talking and listen!

I'm so glad I don't have to take this test again!

Go! Don't look back! Go!

My sister asked me to pass her the chapstick, but I accidentally passed her a glue stick. She still hasn't spoken to me!

I can cut down a tree only using my vision. It's true, I saw it with my own eyes!

Three conspiracy theorists walk into a bar. You can't tell me that's just a coincidence!

So what if I don't know what apocalypse means? It's not the end of the world!

BREEZE THROUGH

Stop! You're ruining my new coat. Or: Stop! You're ruining my new coat!

Maybe now is not the best time.

The seat is mine. Get over it!

I don't know why I couldn't sleep last night.

How exciting! I didn't know Mr Brantley is getting married.

Wow, I simply love it! Or: Wow! I simply love it!

It's a really lovely meal. Thank you.

He's just won the lottery. You don't say!

Come back now!

I still think getting Ann a game was a better idea than a pack of socks.

Unbelievable! The dress was £100! Or: Unbelievable! The dress was £100.

I can see a spider. Quick! Get it out of my bedroom!

Don't bite my arm off! It's only a joke.

It's very peaceful on this side of the hill.

You've managed to do it all in under an hour. That's amazing!

5. Question Mark

LEMON SQUEEZY

Would you mind helping me out?

Of course. Which way did you come in?

What do you call security guards outside the Samsung shop?

Guardians of the Galaxy.

Knock, knock.

Who's there?

Little old lady.

Little old lady who?
I didn't know you could yodel!

Did you hear about the new reversible jackets?
I'm excited to see how they turn out.

Who is the laziest person on earth?
Whoever named the fireplace.

Did you hear about the little girl who went upstairs to get some medicine?
I think she's coming down with something.

Why is the human brain amazing?
It works as soon as you wake up and it doesn't stop until you get to school.

Change is hard.
Have you ever managed to bend a coin?

Mr Morris, why are maths books sad?
I don't know, Alfie. Why are they sad?
Because they have problems to solve.

Did you hear about the kidnapping at school?
It's okay. He woke up.

Isn't it scary that doctors call what they do 'practice'?

Pencils could be made with erasers at both ends, but what would be the point?

What do you call blueberries playing the guitar?
A jam session.

How many months of the year have 28 days?
All of them.

What time is it when 10 elephants are chasing you?
Ten to one.

Did you hear about the hungry clock?
It went back four seconds.

Why is 'abbreviation' such a long word?

Wouldn't exercise be more fun if calories screamed while you burned them?

Don't you hate it when someone answers their own questions?
I do.

Why do seagulls fly over the sea?
Because if they flew over the bay, they'd be bagels.

Why do adults ask children what they want to be when they grow up?
They're looking for ideas.

Am I ambivalent? Well, yes and no.

The teacher said, 'Name two pronouns.'
I said, 'Who? Me?'

What's the difference between a good joke and a bad joke? Timing. (When the joke is written out using correct punctuation, it sadly loses its comical effect; it becomes a fact. If you want people who know punctuation rules to smile when you share it with them, stick to the unpunctuated version – only as a joke because it's then knowingly incorrectly punctuated.)

Why do people believe you when you say there are four billion stars, but check when you say the paint is wet?

Why didn't Noah swat those two mosquitos?

Isn't it amazing that the amount of news that happens around the world every day always exactly fits the newspaper?

Why do banks have their doors open but chain the pens to the counters?

What if there were no rhetorical questions?

6. Listing Comma

OVER TO YOU

1. She's a pretty, fast girl. (B)

2. She's a pretty fast girl. (A)

LEMON SQUEEZY

Chaos, panic, upset, shock and disorder – my work here is done.

Time doesn't exist but wrist watches, pocket watches, kinetic watches, digital watches, analogue watches, wall clocks, Grandpa clocks and all other clocks do.

Remember you are unique, one-of-a-kind, original and completely incomparable – just like everyone else.

Advice for those who don't succeed the first time: stop right there, redefine 'success', redefine 'at first' and destroy all evidence that you've tried.

If you make friends with someone, lend them money, watch them walk away and never see them again – the money was worth it.

I went to Ikea, hid in a wardrobe, waited for the first person to open it and shouted out 'Welcome to Narnia!'

So far, I've visited Birmingham, Manchester, Leeds, Liverpool and York.

We've seen all zoo animals apart from pandas, lemurs, otters, tamarins and elephants.

We had to calculate the cost of four cups of coffee and three cups of tea, check if £15 was enough to pay for all the drinks, work out the ratio between coffee and tea purchased, convert it into a percentage figure, show the findings in a diagram and report to the teacher. *(semicolons could also be used here in place of listing commas)*

Daisy's to-do list included tidying shelves and cupboards, writing a message to Mia, starting a geography homework, calling Grandad in Newport and browsing Amazon for a new pencil case. *(semicolons could also be used here in place of listing commas)*

7. Serial (Oxford) Comma

STEP IT UP

The best fruit are peaches, apples, wild strawberries and blueberries.

My brother is free at the weekend, Monday, and Wednesday. *(he will be working on Tuesday, Thursday and Friday)*

Please may I order today's special deal, cheese, and biscuits? *(cheese and biscuits are two separate items)*

Please may I order today's special deal, cheese and biscuits? *(cheese and biscuits is today's special deal)*

We can't decorate your bedroom without new paint dustsheets, paintbrushes and a ladder.

My historical heroes are the Romans, Julius Caesar and Augustus.

My historical heroes are the Romans, Nelson, and Churchill. *(Nelson and Churchill are not Roman heroes)*

Please could we have two cheeseburgers, one bag of fish fingers, three packets of crisps and three glasses of water?

Don't forget to collect cat food, milk, flour and raspberry jam.

Harriet missed history, design technology and geography lessons because her bus broke down.

Who doesn't like the Queen's corgis, William, and Kate? *(William and Kate are not the names of the Queen's corgis)*

8. Name-Separating Comma

OVER TO YOU

1. Phil the policeman is here. (B) (Bob the builder is a similar phrase)
2. Phil, the policeman is here. (A)

3. Call him Jack and see if he answers. (C)
4. Call him, Jack, and see if he answers. (D)

5. If you like Zoya, I'll leave you. (F)
6. If you like, Zoya, I'll leave you. (E)

7. It's raining cats and dogs. (G)
8. It's raining, cats and dogs. (H)

TAKE A BOW

I'm going bananas. [mad]

I'm going, bananas. [bye]

I don't know, London. [girl]

I don't know London. [city]

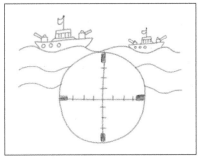

We are sitting ducks. [target]

We are sitting, ducks.

9. Clause the Santa Claus

OVER TO YOU

X	In a nutshell,
CLAUSE	but that **would make** no sense at all!
X	a long, windy road to my village.
CLAUSE	He **wasn't** argumentative.
CLAUSE	which **went down** rather well.
CLAUSE	It **must've been** very frightening for Johnny,
CLAUSE	I immediately **thought** of you.
X	No more for me.
CLAUSE	Unless you **ask**,
X	In reality,
CLAUSE	**Putting** the issues aside,
X	Promptly,
CLAUSE	**Wasn't** it just?
CLAUSE	You **are** welcome.
X	At the top of the stairs,
CLAUSE	**Sit down**, Pudding!
X	However,
X	Michael,
CLAUSE	which **surprised** me.

STEP IT UP

(3) When I **was** a child, my family **moved** a lot, but I always **found** them.

(2) **Take** my advice – I'm (I **am) not using** it.

(2) If **there is** a wrong way to do something, someone **will do** it.

(1) Don't **mention** it, honestly.

(3) Whether Syd **did** it, or Mel **made** him do it, we **will** never **know**.

(2) The dog, which **was left** behind the locked gate, **barked** furiously.

(2) Living on Earth **is** expensive, but it **does include** a free trip around the Sun.

(1) Unbelievably, Paula **was described** as a happy-go-lucky girl.

(2) Ted, who **is** only ten years old, **has** the making of a great chef.

(3) She **told** them that I **didn't know** what I **wanted** for Christmas.

(2) Sienna **shouted** that she **had already been** to that theme park.

(3) The author, who **was** late to the book signing event, **couldn't read** the first chapter because he'd (he **had) forgotten** his glasses.

(2) I **was raised** as an only child, which really **annoyed** my siblings.

(2) Dad **hit** the brake, which **caused** the car to swerve.

(1) In all honesty, I **haven't met** a nicer couple than Jed and Jo.

(3) I **laughed** because the joke she **had told** us **had** the wrong ending.

(3) If you **tell** Nan, I'll **tell** Grandad, and we'll (we **will**) both **be** in trouble.

(2) When your only tool **is** a hammer, all your problems **look** like nails.

10. Commas separating clauses

OVER TO YOU

1. It was a very long zebra crossing. (B)

2. It was a very long zebra, crossing. (A)

3. Save him not, kill him. (C)

4. Save him, not kill him. (D)

5. I'd like building blocks and a puppy for Zeina (F) *(Zeina might be getting building blocks and a puppy, although it's not entirely clear if she gets both)*

6. I'd like building blocks, and a puppy for Zeina (E) *(Zeina is only getting a puppy; I've asked for building blocks for myself)*

11. Main and 'Sub' Clauses

STEP IT UP

If procrastination was an Olympic sport, I'd compete in it later.

When I found out that my toaster wasn't waterproof, I was shocked.

You'll thank me **after** I've done the favour for you.

If every day is a gift, I'd like a receipt for Monday – I want to exchange it for another Friday.

As soon as I try to hug someone cuddly, my face hits the mirror.

If you're not supposed to eat at night, why is there a light bulb in the fridge?

I do unforgettable things **when** I want to improve my memory.

When the past comes knocking, don't answer – it has nothing new to say.

If you run in front of a car, you'll get tired. **If** you run behind the car, you'll get exhausted.

When you're right, no one remembers. **When** you're wrong, no one forgets.

If we have brains to work out problems, why do we use them to create more problems?

Don't look at me **when** I'm trying to concentrate.

If tomatoes are a fruit, is ketchup technically a smoothie?

I stop the microwave one second before the ting **because** I like to feel like a bomb defuser.

When you repeat the same mistakes for so long, you should start calling them traditions.

If you are hotter than me, I am cooler than you.

Chocolate is fruit to me **because** cocoa beans grow on trees.

I like to have a lie in **as long as** I'm allowed to have one.

If a clean desk is the sign of a clear mind, then a clean house is the sign of broken Internet.

When nothing is going right, go left.

Don't stop **when** you're almost there!

If there's the best time to open a gift, it is the present.

When there are footprints on the moon, don't tell me the sky is the limit.

We conveniently forgot to wash Bertie **after** we'd taken him for a walk in a muddy park.

If life is not smiling at you, give it a good tickling.

Emily asked every guest **if** they wanted to sponsor her India expedition.

If you can't convince them, confuse them.

When your children are young, you're a superhero. **When** they're teens, you're a super villain. **After** that, your only power is invisibility.

Although teamwork is overrated, it helps to put the blame on someone else.

If time is money, cash machines should be called time machines.

When in doubt, mumble.

BREEZE THROUGH

Having done her history homework, Aisha went running in the park.

Looking through the glass door, I wondered if the house was empty.

Helped by Gran, I grew impressive tomatoes on the windowsill.

Feeling the pressure, the management removed the 'No dogs' sign.

Having heard it was the teacher's birthday, Sian wrote a poem for Mrs Brown.

Feeling uneasy, I decided not to admit that I never played Minecraft.

Encouraged by all, I made the first step into the unknown.

Having run out of paper, I used my t-shirt to carry on making notes.

Not knowing what to do, we called the reception for help.

Given such an opportunity, of course I was going to take it!

Feeling the cold breeze on my face, I pondered if winter was on its way.

Having practised the routes for months, Marcus was ready for his driving test.

13. Commas 'Hugging' a Subordinate Clause

BREEZE THROUGH

In two weeks, if he takes the medicine regularly, he'll be good as new.

Sam and Kay, feeling exhausted from fixing the computer bug, decided to call it a day.

Abi's biggest secret, if we agree that toddlers can keep secrets, was finally out.

Suri's decision, because she believed in kindness over adventure, was that the dog was reunited with its owner.

Tom's revelation, after he's finally let the cat out of the bag, is that he hates furry animals.

It was Rhona and Geeta who, having completed the first aid course, announced their decision to become army medics.

In hindsight, although my friends begged me, I shouldn't have gone to the party.

My devotion for my dog, after I bought a toddler pushchair for him, was completely slated by other people.

Martha, feeling guilty for what she had done, stood up to make an announcement.

No prizes for guessing, though this is quite a clever Sherlock episode, who the killer is.

The school's parent committee, as long as it's in operation in August, is welcome to attend the event.

Miss Jones' holiday, while we appreciate your concerns, has already been accepted.

Elizabeth, while still grieving her father's death, was crowned the new monarch.

14. Relative Clauses and Puppies

STEP IT UP

✓ People who walk in circles are wondering what they've forgotten.

✗ The bus stop, that we just passed, is always very busy.
(correct: The bus stop that we just passed is always very busy.)

✗ The recipe whom we hadn't tried before is easy to follow.
(correct: The recipe, which we haven't tried before, is easy to follow.)

✓ Ali, who scored four goals, is the new captain of the team.

✓ The jokes that I dislike the most start with 'Knock, knock...'

✗ Mr Blake, which is our neighbour, is a keen gardener.
(correct: Mr Blake, who is our neighbour, is a keen gardener.)

✗ We left Biscuit, that was asleep in his cage, with Mrs Shelley.
(correct: We left Biscuit, who was asleep in his cage, with Mrs Shelley.)

✗ Children, who don't stop smiling, will be let into the tent first.
(correct: Children who don't stop smiling will be let into the tent first.)

✓ The fruit, which we got from Ella, made the cake sweet and rich.

✓ Cold-blooded animals that have scaly skin are called reptiles.

✓ The painting that I forgot to mention in my essay is by Monet.

✗ The answer, that was actually incorrect, earned the team a point.
(correct: The answer, which was actually incorrect, earned the team a point.)

TAKE A BOW
Not all customers are shocked. Only the ones who find out I'm a bad electrician.
✓ Customers who find out I'm a bad electrician are shocked.

I have many books. The one I'm interested in is about anti-gravity.
✓ The book that is about anti-gravity is impossible to put down.

Adam did only one prank and the prank involved swapping tickets.
✓ Adam's prank, which involved swapping tickets, can't be undone.

Although I have many dogs, only my German shepherd guards me at night.
✓ The dog that guards me at night is my German shepherd.

Only one diagnosis was made. It came out of the blue.
✓ The diagnosis, which came out of the blue, was colour blindness.

15. Two or More Main Clauses

OVER TO YOU
Don't ask me anything, and I won't tell you any lies.

Money doesn't grow on trees, yet banks have branches.

Dad and I laugh about how competitive we are, but I laugh more.

I may not have lost all my marbles yet, but there is a small hole in the bag somewhere.

I started out with nothing, and I still have most of it.

A computer once beat me at chess, but it was no match for me at kick boxing.

My pencil supposedly belonged to Shakespeare, but I can't tell if it's 2B or not 2B.

We can't help everyone, but everyone can help someone.

We can watch 'Batman', or we can watch 'Batman Returns'.

I used to think that I was indecisive, but now I'm not too sure.

Never let a fool kiss you, or a kiss fool you.

Cats spend two thirds of their lives sleeping, and the other third making viral videos.

A garage sale is actually a garbage sale, but the 'b' is silent.

Andy's resolution was to read more, so he put the subtitles on TV.

Grandad says he always wanted to be somebody, but he now realised he should have been more specific.

We like birthdays, yet we forget that too many will kill us.

I'd tell you a chemistry joke, but I know I wouldn't get a reaction.

The puzzle said 3–5 years, yet I finished it in 18 months.

You can lead a horse to water, but you can't make it drink.

I wouldn't normally press F5, but it's so refreshing.

The early bird catches the worm, but the second mouse gets the cheese.

It may look like I'm doing nothing, yet in my head I'm very busy.

I'm not saying I'm a superhero, but have you seen me and Batman together in the same place at the same time?

My opinions may have changed, but not the fact that I am right.

Change is inevitable, but not from a vending machine.

16. Commas – Putting It All Together

TAKE A BOW

The maths test, which is actually tomorrow, is too easy to revise for.

After my teacher called me average, I told him it was mean!

People say nothing is impossible, but I do nothing every day.

Lisa, has your missing cat been found yet?

None of my books, which are all arranged alphabetically by the author, is by Dom Harris.

Having burned 3,000 calories, I vowed to never leave cake in the oven while napping.

My opinions may have changed, but not the fact that I'm right.

Rightfully, the man who invented the windowsill is a ledge.

Without ME, even if everyone else was at the party, it was just AWESO.

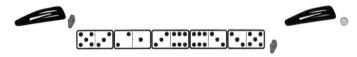

When Dad was a child, family dinners came with two options: take it or leave it.

Run as fast as you can, Loki, and tell everyone Grandad is here.

To be honest, I wanted a fridge magnet, not six new fridges!

Marley sat at the front, so I sat next to him, but Al pretended not to see us.

Ollie opened the door, cautiously looked inside, took his shoes off and tiptoed upstairs.

If you get a letter full of rice, it's from Uncle Ben.

The dog chased the cyclist, making weird noises. (The dog, not the cyclist, was making weird noises.)

The postman, who lives next door, knows our dog really well.

I decided to have Moses, Leah, Seth, Noah, Harry and Aria on my team.

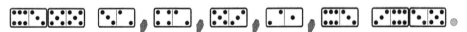

Before long, the secret art project was completed, but Miss Chen had another surprise for us.

I wouldn't say I'm good at athletics, having come last in my class, but I enjoy taking part.

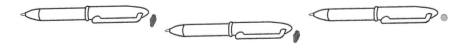

I'd like some Banoffee pie, and ice cream for Freya. (I'd like some Banoffee pie for me, and ice cream for Freya.)

That would never happen, would it?

You ask my opinion, yet you're upset when I give it to you.

Greta Thunberg, whom we never met in person, inspired us the most.

Because the wind is very strong, we're wearing extra layers and raincoats.

After meeting Jaxon, Sian realised what was missing in her life, so she set up a new charity.

Did the shop have carrots, onions, leeks or parsnips?

Because they're always up to something, staircases should never be trusted.

Evening news, although starting with 'Good evening', always leaves people with a worse evening than before they sat down to watch it.

That was my final answer, but the teacher kept asking me more questions.

Listening to a song about a tortilla, Mo knew it was a rap.

Elsie, did you remember to get flour, eggs and milk on the way from school?

If I promise to miss you, will you go now?

The graffiti student, whose name cannot be revealed, called himself the Young Banksy of Merseyside.

Driving too fast, Dad struggled to find the way out.

Shall I do it now, wait until tomorrow, or don't do it at all?

17. Colon

STOP AND THINK
Emoticons' meanings are happy, sad, laughing, cheeky, crying, kiss and unsure.

OVER TO YOU
Secret: something that is told to one person at a time.

Mum's announcement today: 'Happy 10-week anniversary to the 28 browser tabs I have open.'

Anger: the feeling that makes your mouth work faster than your mind.

I was picked for my motivational skills: everyone always says they have to work twice as hard when I'm around.

My teenagers are optimists: every glass they leave around the house is at least half full.

Insanity: doing the same thing over and over again, and expecting different results.

Be a pineapple: stand tall, wear a crown and be sweet on the inside.

To the guy who invented the zero: thanks for nothing!

Determination: taking a lot of steps to avoid lifts.

Some people are like Slinkies: they don't do much all day, but you can't help smiling when you see one tumble down the stairs.

The shinbone: a device for finding furniture in a dark room.

Keep the dream alive: hit the snooze button.

To people who write 'u' instead of 'you': what do you do with all the time you save?

Dad's life complaint: laugh and the world laughs with you, but snore and you sleep alone.

18. Semicolon

STEP IT UP

1. Have a hamster if you can't have a cat. (B)

2. Have a hamster; if you can't, have a cat. (A)

LEMON SQUEEZY

Please buy a suitcase, Levi jacket, vase and a bus ticket. *(commas are used to separate less wordy items in shorter lists)*

Please buy a suitcase big enough to pack all your belongings; a Levi jacket to replace the one you have helped yourself to in my wardrobe; a vase that looks exactly like the one you broke yesterday; and a bus ticket that will take you back to Aunt Jo. *(semicolons are used to separate more wordy items in longer lists)*

BREEZE THROUGH

I explained the word 'many' to my sister; it means a lot to her.

Some people feel the rain; others just get wet.

Knowledge is knowing a tomato is a fruit; wisdom is not putting it in a fruit salad.

I hate insect puns; they really bug me.

Intelligence is like underwear; you need it, but you don't have to show it off.

Or: Intelligence is like underwear: you need it, but you don't have to show it off.

It was the best of times; it was the worst of times.

Entries are wide; exits are narrow.

Our PE teacher has a ticket to the match; he hasn't missed a single game for ten years.

Sometimes I tuck my knees into my chest and lean forward; that's just how I roll.

When I was young, there were only 25 letters in the alphabet; nobody knew why.

I hated my job as an origami teacher; there was too much paperwork.

Or: I hated my job as an origami teacher: there was too much paperwork.

I'm working on a device that will read minds; I'd love to hear your thoughts.

I have two hemispheres: in the left one, there's nothing right; in the right one, there's nothing left.

There are three kinds of people: the ones who learn by reading; the ones who learn by observation; and the rest of them who have to touch the fire to learn it's hot.

19. Dash

BREEZE THROUGH

Not everyone likes maths – no point arguing about that! *(dash)*

It was a short-lived hope. *(hyphen)*

I've found the tickets – it was the best day ever! *(dash)*

The place wasn't just good – it was perfect. *(dash)*

She's such a happy-go-lucky girl. *(hyphens)*

Mum works part-time. *(hyphen)*

What happened was incredible – or so we thought. *(dash)*

At a close-up, it wasn't as scary as we thought it was. *(hyphen)*

I'm just trying to be open-minded about the new bistro. *(hyphen)*

I think – actually, I believe – we should stand up to him. *(dashes)*

LEMON SQUEEZY

I can always tell when my brother is lying – his lips move.

My cousin has just found out I swapped his bed for a trampoline – he hit the roof!

My mother has terrible memory – she never forgets anything!

I decided to take up jogging – especially as it's Lola's favourite sport.

I prefer chocolate to fruity desserts – you can't go wrong with brownies.

All students did well in the rehearsal – the teachers were very excited.

Keep smiling – it makes people wonder what you have been up to!

I heard a voice inside me say, 'Smile! Things could be worse…' so I smiled – and they did get worse.

This is the best rollercoaster you'll ever sit in – hands down.

Everyone everywhere is within walking distance – it only depends on how much time you have.

War doesn't tell us who is right – only who is left.

Grandad said he had never grown up – he had only learned how to act in public.

20. Brackets

OVER TO YOU

The best way to destroy an enemy (apart from a battlefield one) is to make them a friend.

Dad cooked lasagne (my favourite dinner) with four pasta layers.

It's fine if you disagree with me (I can't force you to be right!)

I thought you'd be interested to know (forgive me if you're not) that Aidan has a new girlfriend.

Nobody came to Emma's party, which (you've guessed it) started even earlier than the previous one.

Intelligent people are full of doubt (I think).

If I agreed with you (hypothetically), we'd both be wrong.

Joseph (the boy who has a crush on me) delivers newspapers to our house!

I stood up and hiccupped (that's not weird, is it?)

My French teacher (the one with a motor in her mouth) confused me like I've never been confused before.

Jo's pasta bake (what I prefer to call 'mystery food') went down like a lead balloon.

Reading all sorts of books (apart from Facebook) gives you wisdom in later life.

I loved every moment (and I'm not easily entertained!)

STEP IT UP

Don't just walk in and take my time (unless there's chocolate in your bag).

Or: Don't just walk in and take my time unless there's chocolate in your bag. *(no comma when the main clause is at the front of the sentence)*

The cleverest of all (in my teacher's opinion) is the student who calls themselves a fool at least once a month.

Or: The cleverest of all, in my teacher's opinion, is the student who calls themselves a fool at least once a month.

You are pretty close to perfect (when you're standing next to me).

Or: You are pretty close to perfect when you're standing next to me. *(no comma when the main clause is at the front of the sentence)*

Sometimes the cleverest thing (and you'll know this from experience) is to say nothing at all.

Or: Sometimes the cleverest thing, and you'll know this from experience, is to say nothing at all.

Do you remember John, my sister's boyfriend?

Or: Do you remember John (my sister's boyfriend)?

Myles came to the party. (Do you remember him from school?) He was the real life and soul of the party!

I took a calculated risk (though I'm bad at maths) and it backfired spectacularly.

Or: I took a calculated risk, though I'm bad at maths, and it backfired spectacularly.

I wore my army surplus jacket. (My date thought I looked tidy!)

In moments like this one (when the whole flock is out of order), the farmer sends a distress message to his sheepdog.

Or: In moments like this one, when the whole flock is out of order, the farmer sends a distress message to his sheepdog.

I'll definitely help you with the essay, even though there's no moral ground for it.

Or: I'll definitely help you with the essay (even though there's no moral ground for it).

Barack Obama (the former US president) will be visiting the museum in May.

Or: Barack Obama, the former US president, will be visiting the museum in May.

I've adopted three stick insects. (My brother doesn't know yet!)

My family misbehaved at the party (as always)!

Or: My family misbehaved at the party, as always!

21. Parenthesis

STEP IT UP
After I drank the water, making an awkward gurgling noise, I put the glass down forcefully.

Or: After I drank the water (making an awkward gurgling noise), I put the glass down forcefully.

Or: After I drank the water – making an awkward gurgling noise – I put the glass down forcefully. *(informal)*

Mrs Shirley, who never cooked in her life, was made the Head of Food Tech.

Or: Mrs Shirley (who never cooked in her life) was made the Head of Food Tech.

Zeenat finally turned around (after looking away for two minutes) and explained why the keys had disappeared.

Or: Zeenat finally turned around, after looking away for two minutes, and explained why the keys had disappeared.

I'll do this, though I'm not promising, if I get more free time.

Or: I'll do this (though I'm not promising) if I get more free time.

Or: I'll do this – though I'm not promising – if I get more free time. *(informal)*

I checked the clock (the one on the city hall) before getting on the bus.

Or: I checked the clock – the one on the city hall – before getting on the bus. *(informal)*

Jason (my only Instagram follower) wouldn't do this to me!

Or: Jason – my only Instagram follower – wouldn't do this to me! *(informal)*

Or: Jason, my only Instagram follower, wouldn't do this to me!

I'll get back to you, I hope, tomorrow afternoon.

Or: I'll get back to you – I hope – tomorrow afternoon. *(informal)*

Or: I'll get back to you (I hope) tomorrow afternoon.

We are definitely coming in the summer (more details soon), so we get to meet Sophia in person.

Or: We are definitely coming in the summer – more details soon – so we get to meet Sophia in person. *(informal)*

Miss Rutherford paused (at which point I shut my eyes) before confirming I wasn't allowed to re-sit the test.

Or: Miss Rutherford paused, at which point I shut my eyes, before confirming I wasn't allowed to re-sit the test.

Or: Miss Rutherford paused – at which point I shut my eyes – before confirming I wasn't allowed to re-sit the test. *(informal)*

I looked in the suggested direction (to the right of the post office) but didn't see anything unusual.

Or: I looked in the suggested direction – to the right of the post office – but didn't see anything unusual. *(informal)*

If you have to comment (we know you find it hard not to), at least be fair.

Or: If you have to comment, and we know you find it hard not to, at least be fair.

Or: If you have to comment – we know you find it hard not to – at least be fair. *(informal)*

Play is the most natural activity, right after physiological functions, and should be promoted by teachers and parents.

Or: Play is the most natural activity (right after physiological functions) and should be promoted by teachers and parents.

He didn't run so fast to win the race (perish the thought), though he can be competitive.

Or: He didn't run so fast to win the race, perish the thought, though he can be competitive.

Or: He didn't run so fast to win the race – perish the thought – though he can be competitive. *(informal)*

Being a young child is (without any doubt whatsoever) being a smaller human than an adult.

Or: Being a young child is, without any doubt whatsoever, being a smaller human than an adult.

She was (rather unfortunately) the only candidate we had.

Or: She was, rather unfortunately, the only candidate we had.

Or: She was – rather unfortunately – the only candidate we had. *(informal)*

My dog's counting skills, and I'm being absolutely honest here, are superior to those of my cat.

Or: My dog's counting skills (and I'm being absolutely honest here) are superior to those of my cat.

Or: My dog's counting skills – and I'm being absolutely honest here – are superior to those of my cat. *(informal)*

The family holiday was, all things considered, a resounding success.

Or: The family holiday was (all things considered) a resounding success.

Or: The family holiday was – all things considered – a resounding success. *(informal)*

22. Ellipsis

OVER TO YOU

I like to hold hands at the movies... but it always seems to startle strangers.

I'm just going to flip this omelette... Okay, we're having scrambled eggs.

Your secrets are safe with me... I wasn't even listening.

My friends and I played hide and seek. It went on for hours... Well, good friends are hard to find.

My superpower is making people laugh, which should be great... if I were trying to be funny.

I love my life... but it just wants to be friends.

A bus station is where a bus stops. A train station is where a train stops. On my desk, I have a work station...

23. Hyphen

OVER TO YOU

1. I did twenty four-hour shifts. (C)

2. I did twenty-four hour shifts. (B)

3. I did twenty-four-hour shifts. (A)

STEP IT UP
He is 22 years old and sells old furniture.

He is an old-furniture salesman.

(Aged 22 years old, he is not an old salesman.)

He is not very tall at all, and his job involves writing stories.

He is a short story writer.

(We are not told he only writes short stories.)

She is a holiday rep who works from countries other than UK.

She is an overseas holiday rep.

(We are not told her job is limited to overseas holidays only.)

In his 60s, he is an experienced cheese specialist.

He is a mature cheese expert.

(We are not told his expertise is limited to mature cheese only.)

LEMON SQUEEZY

1. It was a cross section of people. (B)

2. It was a cross-section of people. (A)

3. It was a man hunting beast. (C)

4. It was a man-hunting beast. (D)

STEP IT UP
Dad kissed his little girl good night.

Dad gave his little girl **a good-night kiss**.

This grocery voucher is worth forty pounds.

This is a **forty-pound grocery voucher**.

We never miss the parties at the end of term.

We never miss **end-of-term parties**.

This assignment is well thought out.
This is a **well-thought-out assignment.**

My brother is nine years old.
I have a **nine-year-old brother**.

These clothes are made in a factory.
These are **factory-made clothes**.

Airplanes that fly low create noise pollution.
Low-flying airplanes create noise pollution.

The pattern on his top is eye catching.
His top has an **eye-catching pattern**.

BRING IT ON
These people are **law-abiding citizens**.
These people are law abiding.

I wish she weren't such **a quick-tempered girl**.
I wish she weren't so quick tempered.

What do you do when you meet **a well-known person**?
What do you do when you meet a person who is well known?

Many countries have **a 35-hour working week**.
People work 35 hours per week in many countries.

I'm pleased to reveal **an up-to-date schedule**.
I'm pleased to reveal a schedule that is up to date.

This is a **long-term solution**.
This solution should work in the long term.

Unfortunately, he was described as **a short-fused politician**.
Unfortunately, the politician was described as having a short fuse.

TAKE A BOW
A best friend is like a four-leaf clover: hard to find and lucky to have.
Was the teacher cross-eyed, or she simply couldn't control her pupils?
Waking up this morning was an eye-opening experience.
Teachers who take class register are absent-minded.
Whiteboards are quite re-markable.
Autocorrect should have been named more precisely as autoassume.
A keychain is a device that enables you to lose all keys at once.
The worst things about parallel parking are the eyewitnesses.
If you spent your day in a well, can you say your day was well spent?
I was hoping to steal some leftovers from the party, but I guess my plans were foiled.
Two Wi-Fi antennas got married last Saturday. The reception was fantastic.
I've just been on a once-in-a-lifetime holiday. I'll tell you what, never again!
I thought my neighbours were lovely people. Then they went and put a password on their Wi-Fi.

What does a spy do in the rain? He goes undercover.

The short fortune teller who escaped from prison was a small medium at large.

OVER TO YOU

recreate = give new life or freshness to someone or something (*recreate by regular jogging*)

re-create = form again in the imagination (*re-create the scene in the mind*)

reform = amend or improve something (*reform the educational system*)

re-form = form again (*re-form the blu tack ball*)

24. Inverted commas

OVER TO YOU

1. The policeman said, "The robber was too quick." (B)

2. "The policeman," said the robber, "was too quick." (A)

LEMON SQUEEZY
In all examples below, use of either single or double inverted commas is correct as long as they are used consistently within the same sentence or passage.

My neighbour used to say, "As one door closes, another opens."

Such a lovely man, but a terrible cabinet maker.

"Dogs are easily amused", thought Sam while watching her dog chase his tail. She then realised that she was watching her dog chase his tail.

I put the 'pro' in procrastinate.

Don't spell 'part' backwards – it's a trap!

Whoever invented 'Knock knock' jokes should get a 'No bell' prize.

When you just slipped and fell, simply say, "Yep, gravity still works!"

I'm all for irony, but the phrase 'Good morning' is proving a bit too far.

Pool rule: you're not allowed to do anything that begins with the words: "Hey everyone, watch this!"

Does anyone actually know what the 'I'm feeling lucky' button on Google page means?

Most of the year: "I want this, I want that!" Near my birthday: "I can't think of a single thing I want."

Teachers use words, such as 'creative' and 'strong-willed' to describe Esme. We simply think she is stubborn.

If you send a text message saying, 'I heard what you said about me', you could find out rather a lot about what the person thinks about you.

Did you know that if you hold your ear up to a stranger's knee, you can actually hear them say, "What do you think you are doing?"

Sometimes, when I am matching socks, I'm horrified to think, 'What if these two socks don't even like each other?'

I saw a doctor about my hearing problem. He asked, "Can you describe the symptoms?" I said, "Homer is fat, Marge has blue hair, Maggie has the brains and Bart is a real nightmare."

I like to give people blank 'Thank you' cards for their birthdays. When they ask me what they're for, I say, "You'll thank me later!"

Doctor: "Sir, I'm afraid your DNA is backwards." Me: "And?"

People used to laugh at me when I would announce, 'I want to be a comedian!' Well, nobody's laughing now.

I got my sister a 'Get better soon' card. She's not sick – I just think she could get better.

Maggie pleaded, "Please eat the broken biscuits first because I feel so bad for them."

Dads everywhere: 'Don't worry, kids. Mum just turned the car radio down, so we shouldn't be lost much longer.'

'What's an essay conclusion, Jamie?'

'That part where you're tired of thinking.'

Text to Mum: "I'll be there in 5 minutes. If not, read this message again."

I was complimented on my fine driving. Someone left a 'Parking Fine' note.

A man went to the doctor's and said, "I've hurt my arm in several places." The doctor said, "Well, don't go there any more."

Teacher: 'You missed school yesterday.'

Joe: 'To tell you the truth, I didn't really miss it.'

I read recipes the same way I read sci-fi stories: I get to the end and think, "Well, that's not going to happen!"

25. Possessive Apostrophe

BREEZE THROUGH
Mum's stories are very funny, but not when she jokes about Pebbles' first encounter with the vet.

Windows are really TVs for cats.

If you step on someone's foot, they open their mouth like a bin.

From the chairs' viewpoint, humans are mainly bums.

Which country's capital is the fastest growing? Ireland's. Every year it's Dublin.

These are children's books; dictionaries are over there.

Molly's dream was to never have spinach flan ever again.

I have two baby sisters and the babies' cots are right next to my bed.

Men's coats are to your left, and women's shoes are on the first floor.

Mr Spark was asked to park in the visitors' car park.

Dad's boss's pen was in his pocket.

We could ask Adam's brother to babysit for us.

If you want to stop an astronaut's baby from crying, you rocket.

A vampire's favourite fruit is obviously a blood orange.

Mr Norman's message on the school's website: 'To the student who stole my glasses. I will find you. I have contacts.'

How many musicians does it take to screw in a lightbulb? And a one, and a two, and a three...

You can tell an ant's gender by putting it in water: sinks – girl ant, floats – buoyant.

BRING IT ON
THOMPSON'S BAKERY

No barbeques allowed on the field

NO TAXIS. RESIDENTS' CARS ONLY.

Hot drinks served here

NOTICE Toilets to the right

CARS PARKED AT OWNERS' RISK

St Mary's Children's Hospital

26. Contracting Apostrophe

OVER TO YOU
who's is short for **who is** or **who has**

whose is asking '**Who does this belong to?**'

BREEZE THROUGH

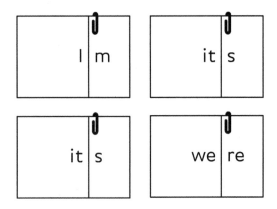

LEMON SQUEEZY

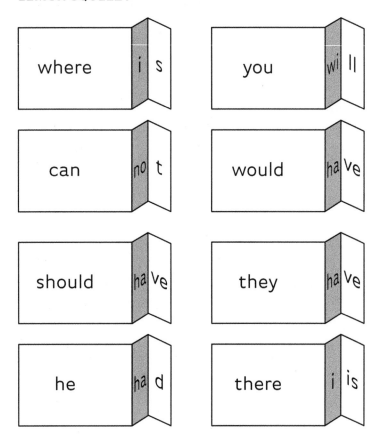

BREEZE THROUGH

it's = it is, or it has

I'm = I am

you'll = you will

wasn't = was not

could've = could have

we're = we are

they've = they have

can't = cannot

mustn't = must not

he'd = he would, or he had

aren't = are not

hadn't = had not

wouldn't = would not

should've = should have

won't = will not

might've = might have

shan't = shall not

they're = they are

who's = who is, or who has

hasn't = has not

there's = there is

couldn't = could not

weren't = were not

didn't = did not

STEP IT UP

She'll sell a shell by the seashore.

The shell she'll sell will be very well wrapped.

We're aware that you were away.

Were we not aware you're away, we wouldn't worry we're on our own.

The shed she'd bought needed some shade.

She'd better get the shed that she'd planned to buy.

We'll write to you about the well well in time.

Don't change the price, or we'll change our mind about the well.

TAKE A BOW

It's (It is) a 30-minute walk from my house to the school, but a 10-minute walk back home. **I'd (I would)** say **it's (it is)** a mystery!

I've (I have) had a row with my boss at lunchtime – one of the perks of working near a boating lake.

It's (It is) so annoying when people get their sayings wrong. After all, **it's (it is)** not rocket salad!

No matter how enraged Germaine Greer gets, **she'll (she will)** never be as furious as her sister, Anne.

Finding my lost luggage at the airport is a nightmare. You might think **it'd (it would)** be easy, but **that's (that is)** not the case.

My boyfriend found a pile of letters **I'd (I had)** hidden and accused me of cheating. He said **he'd (he would)** never play scrabble with me again.

I've (I have) done my first ever book signing. **I'm (I am)** now banned from the library.

I **don't (do not)** see the point of a pocket calculator. Who **doesn't (does not)** know how many pockets they have?

Who's (Who is) in charge of the hankies? The handkerchief.

I'd (I had) bought rocket salad, but **it's (it has)** gone off before I could eat it.

To be Frank, **I'd (I would)** have to change my name.

He's (He has) quit his job at the helium factory today. **He's (He is)** not being spoken to in that tone of voice!

27. How to Solve a Problem like Zed?

OVER TO YOU
Correct answers:

1. When I close my eyes, I can't see.

2. I could've done it if I'd tried harder.

3. Ollie's brothers' choice was to sell their shares in the company.

4. It's not true all of our teachers' worries are students' grades.

5. Tolkien famously said, "Not all those who wander are lost."

6. Having played in Manchester, the band is coming to our city.

7. The team struggled to communicate; we lost the game.

8. I'm off, Lily. Please feed Scratch, Clawsby, Catzilla and Pud.

9. Just as I finished, it started raining, which ruined my project.

10. Children's parties are welcome here.

11. The full amount, first requested in June, is yet to be paid.

12. With the exception of one hiccup, the lesson went rather well.

13. The new teacher, who looks like Doctor Who, is our form tutor.

14. According to Mr Frost, the students worked 'exceptionally hard'.

15. Who's left their jacket behind?

16. Jo's second-hand car theft account seemed a far-fetched story.

Completed activation key: WINNINGHANDSDOWN (winning hands down).

BRING IT ON
Why We Need Punctuation
Thanks for helping, Billy. Get out of the house!

You can't read punctuation marks.

Capital Letter
I have a proper name.

I say, 'Be somebody nobody thought you could be.'

I know a human as mad as a March hare!

Thirty days has September. All the rest I can't remember...

I was made in China, so a part of me is Chinese.

Or 'How to Build a Robot' by Cy Borg.

Haven't you read the book by Peter Brown?

Dogs with wet noses hurt more than bad landing.

They interfere with my electric circuits.

Is 'Star Wars' a title or a brand name? Asking for R2-D2...

Full Stop
'Cross' and 'disappointed' are negative emotions.

I will (full) stop at nothing.

Question Mark
Why only questions?

No question marks in my programing language.

I don't like homework with question marks.

Good on Dad!

Listing Comma
She is a monster!

I can't see any commas in the pot.

Serial (Oxford) Comma
Nobody told me Lady Gaga and Ed Sheeran had a child.

My name is Zed, not Alexa.

Name-Separating Comma
Because I'm funny?

Humans say one thing and mean a trouble.

I know trouble when I hear one.

The wolf has shrunk the children!

Clause the Santa Claus
Claws-is?

Robots are good heads; they solve problems faster.

The doing word.

Clause sounds like Santa Claus.

The comma helps to avoid conclusion.

Main and 'Sub' Clauses
After the teacher said it was a piece of cake...

Timmy ate his homework.

What joke?

Makes no sense.

Dogs eat homework.

'Subordinate' is a long word.

Unless you want your writing to sink to the bottom of the sea.

Comma after Fronted Adverbials
Fronted mousers are lazy, so they have no doing words.

I knew Santa wouldn't have anything to do with mousers.

Robots will time travel before humans.

Commas 'Hugging' a Subordinate Clause
Hugging is overrated. You can get an electric shock.

Relative Clauses and Puppies
The human who broke the robot kept pushing all the buttons.

Two out of three humans in every electronics shop.

Two or More Main Clauses
I can see ships, but not a single submarine.

Commas – Putting It All Together
Plain English, please!

Approaching System Overload Error!

Colon
If you know what :/ mean.

You said they were emoticons.

Semicolon
'Consecutive' means one after another.

Why look at me?

Dash
If I had a stomach, it would be turning right now.

All clear. Gotta dash now! *(informal)*

Brackets
He is an important person.

But he is closest to the rain clouds.

So I read the extra words for nothing?

And ask for a weather forecast for next week.

This does not apply if your punctuation software update is delayed.

Give a robot the right software, and it will give one hundred per cent.

Parenthesis
All you need is love.

'Looking dapper' is in brackets.

Ellipsis
Or trying to send unfinished SOS messages.

Hyphen
Why not 'hy-phenated'?

Smarty-pants students alert!

So why bother with hyphens?

Inverted Commas
Finally, a ghost story!

Possessive Apostrophe
A friendly reminder: I have no thumbs.

Contracting Apostrophe

Alert in my data analysis: the folding device doesn't work for all contractions!

No Wi-Fi.

Challenge accepted.

How to Solve a Problem like Zed?

Got what?

I'd rather have a zillion system bugs than sound like Alexa.

Threat detected. Evacuate! Evacuate! Evacuate!

28. Zed Has the Last Word

OVER TO YOU

The dog chased a man on a bicycle.

Who was on the bicycle: the dog or the man?

I saw her duck.

Did she show you her domesticated water bird, or did you see her lower her head or body forward to avoid getting hit by something?

Free whales!

Are the whales free to go to a good home? Or are we campaigning to release them from captivity?

Look at the cat with one eye.

Are you asking me to close one eye when looking at the cat, or does the cat have only one eye?

I saw the man with the telescope.

Did you use the telescope to look at the man, or did you see him carry or look through the telescope?

The vicar married my niece.

Was the vicar the official who married the couple, or was he the groom?

They fed her rat poison.

Did they poison her, or did they use the poison that belonged to her?

Visiting relatives can be boring.

Are relatives who come for visits boring, or is visiting the relatives a boring activity?

He loves the hamster more than his wife.

Who loves the hamster more: he or his wife? Or does his love for his wife come second after that for the hamster?

The puppy sat by the girl with the pleased look.

Who had the pleased look: the puppy or the girl?

Call me a taxi.

Okay, you're a taxi. Or shall I get you a taxi to take you to your destination?

Giant waves down Queen Mary's funnels.

Does this newspaper title refer to a major disturbance on the surface of the sea that affected the ship's funnels? Or was there a massive superhuman-looking creature waving down the ship's funnels?

Further Reading

Specialist reference

Brown, G., Currie, K.L and Kenworthy, J. (2015) *Questions of Intonation*. Abingdon: Routledge.

Oxford University Press (2013) *Oxford School Spelling, Punctuation and Grammar Dictionary*. Oxford: Oxford University Press.

Oxford University Press (2014) *Oxford Primary Grammar, Punctuation and Spelling Dictionary*. Oxford: Oxford University Press.

Quirk, R., Greenbaum, S., Leech, G. and Svartvik, J. (1990) *A Comprehensive Grammar of the English Language*. London: Longman.

Punctuation facts

Cathill, P. (2017) Interesting Histories: Comma, Dot, Question Mark & Exclamation Mark. *Medium online*. Available at: https://medium.com/interesting-histories/interesting-histories-comma-dot-question-mark-exclamation-mark-90efb9300bfa, accessed on 04 November 2019.

Cook, V.J. (2013) 'Standard Punctuation and the Punctuation of the Street.' In M. Pawlak and L. Aronin (eds) *Essential Topics in Applied Linguistics and Multilingualism*. Switzerland: Springer International Publishing.

Cook, V.J. (2019) Frequencies for English Punctuation Marks. Available at: www.viviancook.uk/Punctuation/PunctFigs.htm, accessed on 18 November 2019.

Houston, K. (2015) The Mysterious Origins of Punctuation. *BBC Culture*. Available at: www.bbc.com/culture/story/20150902-the-mysterious-origins-of-punctuation, accessed on 04 November 2019.

General reference

BBC Newsround (2019) *What is Ramadan*? Available at: www.bbc.co.uk/newsround/23286976, accessed on 04 November 2019.

Dickens, C. (2016) *Great Expectations*. London: MacMillan Collector's Library.

Grammarist (2019) *Emoji vs Emoticon*. Available at: https://grammarist.com/new-words/emoji-vs-emoticon, accessed on 04 November 2019.

Lambert, T. (2019) A Brief History of Clocks and Calendars. *Local Histories*. Available at: www.localhistories.org/clocks.html, accessed on 04 November 2019.

National Geographic Kids (2019) *Facts about Diwali*. Available at: www.natgeokids.com/uk/discover/geography/general-geography/facts-about-diwali, accessed on 04 November 2019.

Owano, N. (2012) 'Kawaii' Power Sharpens Worker Focus, says Japanese Study. *Medical Press*. Available at: https://medicalxpress.com/news/2012-10-kawaii-power-sharpens-worker-focus.html, accessed on 04 Novembe 2019.

Soft Schools (2019) *Easter Facts*. Available at: www.softschools.com/facts/holidays/easter_facts/153/, accessed on 04 November 2019.

Stewart, W. and Engel, C. (2019) *What Do You Celebrate? Holidays and Festivals Around the World*. New York: Sterling Children's Books.

The Fact File (2019) *99 Interesting Facts about Christmas*. Available at: www.thefactfile.org/interesting-facts-christmas, accessed on 04 November 2019.

Travel China Guide (2019) *10 Facts You Should Know about Chinese New Year*. Available at: https://www.travelchinaguide.com/essential/holidays/new-year/facts.htm, accessed on 04 November 2019.

Jokes and humorous content

Ellis, M. (2008) *The Little Book of Jokes for Kids of All Ages*. Newcastle: Zymurgy Publishing.

Pocket Pal (2009) *Jokes to Tell*. Heatherton: Hinkler Books.

Wicked Uncle (2019) *Joke Factory*. Available at: www.wickeduncle.co.uk/jokes, accessed on 18 November 2019.

by the same author

Tricky Spelling in Cartoons for Children
Lidia Stanton

of related interest

Dyslexia is My Superpower (Most of the Time)
Margaret Rooke

Fun Games and Activities for Children with Dyslexia
How to Learn Smarter with a Dyslexic Brain
Alais Winton

The Dyslexia, ADHD and DCD-Friendly Study Skills Guide
Tips and Strategies for Exam Success
Ann-Marie McNicholas

How Can I Remember All That?
Simple Stuff to Improve Your Working Memory
Dr Tracy Packiam Alloway

The Self-Help Guide for Teens with Dyslexia
Useful Stuff You May Not Learn at School
Alais Winton

Index